D0374845

Murrieta Hot Springs Vegetarian Cookbook

by the
Murrieta
Foundation

Revised and Expanded
including Spa Cuisine

The Book Publishing Company   •   Summertown, Tennessee 38483

Contributing Editors:
Jane Buck
John Chitty
Judith Handelsman
Dolores Ransom
Susan Strathairn

And thanks to all the Murrieta Foundation Staff

On the Cover: Adventurer's Kabobs *(pg. 204) with Salad and Tropical Fruit Plate (pg. 189), Photographer: Michael Bonnickson, Food Stylist: Louise Hagler*

On the Back Cover: Photographer: Steven Simpson, Food Stylists: Jim Bunch, Jane Buck, Susan Strathairn, Barbara Maynord, Grounds Photographer: Mark Allison

1 2 3 4 5 6 7 8 9 0   Printed in the US by R.R. Donnelley & Sons,

©1987 The Book Publishing Company, Summertown, TN 38483

ISBN 0-913990-54-X

Library of Congress Cataloging-in-Publication Data
Murrieta Hot Springs vegetarian cookbook: including spa cuisine / by
  the Murrieta Foundation.
      p.   cm.
  Includes index.
  ISBN 0-913990-54-X: $9.95
  1. Vegetarian cookery. I. Murrieta Foundation (Murrieta, Calif.)
TX837.M87 1987
641.5'636—dc19   87-21881
                                                                 CIP

2

CONTENTS

PART II

Vegetarian Cuisine From Murrieta Hot Springs

Introduction

Healthy eating is a way of life which can enhance every aspect of living. Here at Murrieta Hot Springs, the largest vegetarian spa and restaurant in the country, we have years of experience in cooking, serving and enjoying delicious, healthful diets.

This cookbook presents vegetarian recipes for all occasions. Included are delicious gourmet recipes as well as purifying and cleansing ideas. Whether you are just discovering vegetarian eating or are an old timer, this book is for you. In this introduction you will find useful back-ground information for general diet planning as well as weight loss dieting from our "Fit 'N Trim" Program.

We believe that the vegetarian way of life is a foundation for balanced living on all levels. We teach the physical, emotional, mental and spiritual benefits of becoming a vegetarian, but you don't have to be a vegetarian to enjoy these recipes.

A Few Words About Murrieta Hot Springs

Located in the peaceful Temecula Valley north of San Diego, California, Murrieta Hot Springs is a perfect place for rest and renewal. Forty-six acres of landscaped paradise await the seeker of health and relaxation. This is a place where all details are planned with health in mind. The resort serves only lacto-vegetarian foods, excludes alcohol or smoking, and provides a wide range of exercise, natural health theory, and bodywork classes. There are also sports (tennis, swimming and golf) and entertainment (live stage theater performances) for the whole family.

At the heart of the resort are our health programs. These residential courses for self-discovery and growth range from weekend seminars to our comprehensive four-week Basic Program. These classes survey the entire field of holistic health. Guests enjoy services at the hot mineral springs spa, vegetarian meals in the Oasis Buffet, and valuable classes summarizing ancient and modern knowledge on health and well-being. We particularly emphasize the significance of family harmony, stress management and effective communication skills. Then we add the physical aspects of diet and exercise to create a total health experience.

Using Food For Health Benefits

It's well known by now how much food affects our health. We know that foods have the ability to build the body, facilitate cleansing, and stabilize or sensitize emotions. In our programs we use three diets as taught by Dr. Randolph Stone D.C., D.N., D.O. (1890-1982), founder of Polarity Therapy. These three diets called *Purifying, Health-Building,* and *Gourmet Vegetarian,* offer broad and easily-understood principles for effective food management. In this book you'll find each recipe identified by its diet classification.

Before we go into the descriptions of each diet, we'd like to mention a little bit about attitude. *How we feel* as we eat can be as significant as *what we eat.* Take time to enjoy the processes of creating and serving, eating and digesting your food. The best-planned diet can be undermined by hasty and disorderly preparation. Come to your kitchen and table with a calm attitude of thankfulness. Love and serenity are the ultimate condiments!

Let's also mention transitions. When making a change in diet (for instance, when moving from Purifying to Health-Building) take moderate, gradual steps. Add one food each day, and evaluate the effect of that change. Obviously, different people will notice different sensitivities and needs. You can profit by knowing your own limitations. This is especially true for vegetarians, who can expect to become increasingly sensitive as time goes by.

The Three Diets

The Purifying Diet is designed to promote internal cleansing. The bloodstream becomes alkaline and accumulated toxins leave the body. Because these foods are easily digestible, they accelerate the digestive process and promote cleansing. *The Purifying Diet* is useful for weight loss programs and for periodic revitalizing and cleansing.

Foods on the Purifying Diet	Foods to Avoid on the Purifying Diet
Cooked and raw vegetables	Dairy Products
Sprouted seeds and legumes	Grains
Fresh and dried fruits	Unsprouted beans or legumes
Wheatgrass juice	Sugar
Vitality Drink	Salt
Polari-Tea	Nuts and nut butters
Essene bread	Breads, cakes, pastries, etc.
Cold-pressed oils (except corn)	Potatoes
Yams and avocados	Foods containing caffeine
Honey and fructose	Vinegar
Soaked almonds	

Sample Purifying Menu

Day One

Breakfast
Vitality Drinks(pg. 21)
Polari-Tea (pg. 21)

Lunch
Soy Burgers with trimmings on
  Essene toast (pg. 97)
Ketchup (pg. 36)
Carrot Raisin Crunch Salad
  (pg. 62)

Dinner
Vegetable Pizza (pg. 96)
Fresh Spinach Salad (pg. 62)
Minestrone Soup (pg. 55)

Day Two

Breakfast
Orange Almond Cream Sauce
  (pg. 52) over pears, apples, and
  soaked almonds
Apple Juice

Lunch
Vegetable Pizza (pg. 96)
Mixed Sprout Salad (pg. 63)

Dinner
Baked Harvest Vegetables
  (pg. 98)
Stuffed Artichokes (pg. 94)
Tossed Salad
Golden Italian Dressing
  (pg. 70)
Lemon Coconut Dream Pie
  No. 2 (pg. 117) on Purifying Pie
  Crust (pg. 112)

The Health-Building Diet is a foundation for general daily nutrition, emphasizing food combinations which are easily digestible.

Sample Health Building Menu

Day One

Breakfast
Cooked Millet with Butter
  (pg. 16)
Almonds and Maple Syrup
Whole wheat toast (oil-free)
  with Better Butter (pg. 35)
  or Butter
Polari-Tea (pg. 21)

Lunch
Curried Sprouted Lentils (pg. 91)
Acorn Squash Chutney (pg. 34)
Fresh Yogurt
Whole wheat Flour Tortillas
  (oil-free)
Condiments: Coconut, Raisins,
  Green Chilies, Red Chili Seeds

Dinner
Rice and Vegetable Nori Rolls
  (pg. 94)
Guacamole (pg. 37)
Fresh Zucchini & Cucumber
  Sticks

Day Two

Breakfast
Angel Sauce
Sliced Apples, Pears, Bananas or
  any other in-season fruit
Raisin Essene Toast

Lunch
Tofu Salad in Tomato Flower
  (pg. 175)
Gazpacho (pg. 58)

Dinner
Chinese Tofuey (pg. 86)
Sprouted Brown Rice (pg. 18)
Tossed Salad with Sunflower
  Seeds
Orange Ice Freeze (pg. 122)

Good Food Combinations	*Combinations to Avoid*
All proteins together All starches together	Starches with Proteins, such as: Grains or potatoes with unsprouted beans or tofu
Grains and sweet fruits	Grains or potatoes with nuts (except soaked almonds)
Starches and dairy foods	Starches and acidic foods, such as: grains or
Proteins and acidic foods	Potatoes with citrus fruits, tomatoes or vinegar
Dairy and sweet fruits	

Foods on the Health-Building Diet	Foods to Avoid on the Health-Building Diet
All foods on the Purifying List Whole grains, rice, wheat, etc. Unheated milk products Raw nuts and nut/seed butters Potatoes, beans, nutritional yeast	Cooked Cheese Heated oils and butters Roasted nuts, seeds, nut butters Baked goods with oil or butter Fried foods & refined foods, such as, sugar, white or unbleached flour, white rice

The Gourmet Vegetarian Diet is a general diet for special occasions and for people with hearty appetites and physically demanding schedules. This diet tends to have some factors which are not considered ideal for long-term consumption, including higher fat content, more salt and sweeteners, and such dishes as fried foods. Here the emphasis is on satisfaction and contentment, an important part of your overall dining experience.

Our *Gourmet Vegetarian Diet* includes all lacto-vegetarian foods. As always the emphasis is on fresh, pure ingredients and loving preparation.

Sample Gourmet Vegetarian Menu

Day One

Breakfast
Honey Granola (pg. 30)
Fresh Yogurt with Sliced
    Strawberries & Bananas
Orange Juice

Lunch
Tofu Tidbits (pg. 84)
Tartar Sauce (pg. 46)
Smokey Lentil Soup (pg. 57)
Carrot & Celery Sticks

Dinner
Murrieta Enchilada (pg. 74)
Sopa de Mexico (pg. 56)
Corn Chips
Mexican Salsa (pg. 46)

Day Two

Breakfast
Breakfast Tofu (pg. 26)
Whole Wheat Croissant with
    Butter or Better Butter (pg. 35)

Lunch
Cottage Rolls (pg. 79)
Split Pea Soup (pg. 54)

Dinner
Spinach Quiche (pg. 75)
French Onion Soup (pg. 58) with
    Croutons & Parmesan Cheese
Steamed Brocolli with Savory
    Sauce (pg. 42)
Tossed Green Salad & Thousand
    Island Salad Dressing (pg. 66)
Raspberry Jelly Rolls No. 2
    (pg. 103)

Description of Key Ingredients

Agar (flakes or granulated) - A tasteless seaweed, used as a gelatin or pectin substitute. We use it mainly in our desserts and fruit jells. Other uses are in soups, salads, jams and puddings.

Arrowroot Powder - Used as a more delicate thickener in place of flour or cornstarch. Arrowroot is a nutritious food which is actually a powdered root. We use it mostly in gravies and sauces.

Polari-Tea - This delightful herbal blend contains flax, fenugreek, licorice, peppermint and fennel. Its naturally sweet taste and soothing qualities make this caffeine-free tea a family favorite. Ask for *Polari-Tea* at your health food store or write to us.

Better Butter - Lower in cholesterol and very tasty, *Better Butter* contains butter, almond oil and lecithin spread. See recipe on page 35.

Carob - Ground from the carob pod, this sweet powder has a flavor similar to chocolate and contains no caffeine.

Egg Replacer - A combination of starches and leavening agents, egg replacer leavens and acts as a binder in cooked and baked foods.

Fructose - We use fructose as the main sweetener in our restaurant. Fructose provides a steady energy which feeds the brain and nervous system with less of the sudden and stressful surges of energy resulting from glucose or sucrose. Substitute honey to taste (usually a good gauge is less honey to fructose). For example, for 1 cup fructose use ¾ cup honey. Also, use less liquid in the recipe to compensate for texture changes.

Ghee - In the Far East, ghee is used just as butter is used in the West. In ghee, the heavier solids and butter fat have been removed, making it easier to digest after being subjected to high temperatures. See recipe on page 32. Substitute the same amount of butter or any oil as ghee. In melted ghee recipes, use almond oil in sweet recipes and safflower oil or olive oil in savory recipes. Walnut oil and apricot oil both have a delicate taste but tend to be expensive. Use any vegetable oil you like in any recipe except olive oil, which does not taste good in sweet dishes.

Gluten Flour - Made from whole wheat, this is the protein left over when the starch has been removed. It is very concentrated and gives an elastic quality in cooking.

Lecithin Spread - This cholesterol-free spread is available in most health food stores. We use it in making Better Butter and in several other recipes.

Liquid Aminos - This is a liquid mineral-soy bouillon with a wonderful and distinctive flavor. We use it in the cooking of soups and main dishes or sprinkled over steamed vegetables or grains. For substitution, dilute ½ Tamari and ½ water, or use sea salt to taste, or vege-salt to taste (watch out, these can be very salty).

Miso - Rich in B vitamins and enzymes, this soybean paste has been fermented and aged. It adds a distinctive flavor to soups and sauces. Add miso after your dish has been taken off high heat in order to retain its high vitamin content. Substitute ½ tsp. of sea salt for 1 Tbsp. miso.

Tahini - This is a sesame seed butter with a nutty, bitter-sweet flavor that is used extensively in the Middle East.

Tamari - Aged naturally, this concentrated soy sauce contains no sugar. It's great for cooking and can be used on steamed vegetables, grains or potatoes. Substitute sea salt to taste, or use approximately twice as much liquid aminos.

Tempeh - Like tofu, tempeh is made from soy and is a complete protein. It has been fermented from whole soybeans and pressed. Its texture lends itself to hearty foods and entrees.

Tofu - This incredibly versatile, high-protein food is low in calories, fats and carbohydrates and has no cholesterol. We use it in our restaurant in everything from quiche to desserts. Tofu is a soybean curd and is a very receptive ingredient, picking up the flavors of other foods.

Umeboshi Plums - These pickled and salted plums are imported from Japan. They are excellent in oriental dishes. Substitute sea salt to taste.

Varietal Grape Juices - Look in your store's gourmet section for these fine, delicious non-alcoholic grape juices made from specific varieties. These are not to be confused with the common purple Concord grape product.

Watch Out For
Hidden Non-Vegetarian Ingredients

Being a vegetarian offers tremendous health benefits on all levels. It is well worth the effort to watch for these common foods which frequently contain non-vegetarian ingredients. Clear guidelines, and a little research and label-reading go a long way.

Below is a list of foods to watch out for while traveling, eating out, or grocery shopping:

Gelatin (from horses' hoofs) is often in: ricotta cheese, jelly beans, marshmallows, candies, yogurt, jello, sour cream, ice cream

Lard or "Animal Shortening" is often in: pie crusts, muffin, biscuit and cakemixes, crackers, breads, ice cream cones, cereals, Mexican foods such as beans and enchilada sauce, and flour tortillas

Eggs are often found in: breads, mayonnaise, ice cream (such as French Vanilla), salad dressings, root beer, potato salad, noodles, candy bars, baked goods, such as: noodles, cakes, donuts and cookies, pizza crust, bakery glazes, pancakes, "orange julius" drinks

Glandular extracts or pancreatin are sometimes found in vitamins and food supplements.

Oysters are in: oyster sauces in Chinese dishes.

Chicken or Beef Bouillon is often in: soups, pizza sauce, casseroles, Chinese dishes

In restaurants, fried potatoes and onion rings are often cooked in animal shortening or in oil which has been used for cooking chicken or fish. Also, check to see if your vegetarian order will be cooked on the same grill as non-vegetarian foods.

Vegetarian Starter Kit

The Basics
GRAINS:
- [ ] Rice, 3 lbs. [ ] Millet, 2 lbs.
- [ ] Oats, 1 lb.[ ] Popcorn, 2 lbs.

BEANS:
- [ ] Pinto Beans, l lb.
- [ ] Lentils, 1 lb.[ ] Canned Chili
- [ ] Canned Garbanzos/Kidneys (watch label for sugar)
- [ ] Bean Dip (watch for lard)

TOFU:
- [ ] 1 Pkg. - 1 or 2 per week

NOODLES:
- [ ] Sesame [ ] Soy or [ ] Spinach
- [ ] Artichoke (De Boles), 1 lb.

SPAGHETTI SAUCE:
- [ ] Johnson's™ - 6 jars

NUTS:
- [ ] Almonds, 1 lb.[ ] Sunflower Seeds, 1 lb.
- [ ] Cashews, 1 lb.[ ] Sesame Seeds, 1 lb.

NUT BUTTERS:
- [ ] Almond Butter, 2 lbs.[ ] or Tahini or Cashew

ALMOND OIL (Hains Cold-Pressed™):
- [ ] 2 bottles
- [ ] or Safflower (cheaper) [ ] or Sesame

LIQUID AMINOS:
- [ ] Dilute ½ Strength with Water (if concentrated)

NORI:
- [ ] 1 Pkg.

VEGETABLES:
- [ ] Fresh-organic when possible

DRIED FRUIT:
- [ ] Raisins, 1 lb. or Apricots,
- [ ] Peaches, Apples, Bananas or Figs

ALFALFA SPROUTS:
- [ ] or ¼ lb. Alfalfa Seeds

FRUCTOSE:
- [ ] ½ lb. (100% − Fructose 90)

GRANOLA:
- [ ] 2lbs.

DAIRY:
- [ ] Cheese, Sour Cream, Yogurt
- [ ] Cottage Cheese, Milk, etc.

VINEGAR:
- [ ] Apple Cider, 1qt.

**Remember to read labels to check for:*
Eggs, Lard, Gelatin, Albumen (Egg White).

Prepared Foods (Check your Health Food Store for more ideas)
FALAFEL MIX
CHOPPED CANNED OLIVES
HOT SAUCE
CANNED SOUPS:
- [ ] Read labels**

TOFU BURGERS:
- [ ] 1 Pkg. (1 or 2 per week)

MAYONNAISE:
- [ ] Eggless (Hain's)

SALAD DRESSING (Eggless)
POLARI-TEA

Breads
WHOLE WHEAT ENGLISH MUFFINS AND CHAPATTIS
CORN TORTILLAS
PITA BREAD
ESSENE BREAD: Lifestream™
Any WHOLE GRAIN BREAD:
- [ ] Without eggs (Food for Life makes Rye, Ezekiel, etc...)

For Baking
MILK POWDER
- [ ] non-instant

WHOLE WHEAT FLOUR:
- [ ] for bread

WHOLE WHEAT PASTRY FLOUR:
- [ ] for other baking

CAROB POWDER, ARROWROOT, AGAR
LECITHIN SPREAD, EGG REPLACER (Ener-G™)

Spices
THYME, BASIL, ONION POWDER
OREGANO,GARLIC POWDER, CAYENNE

Sample Protein Drink
MILK	2 cups
MALT POWDER	1 Tbsp.
FRUCTOSE	1 Tbsp.
PROTEIN POWDER	1 Tbsp.
Fruit or Vanilla, if desired	

Pots - Basic Needs
(avoid aluminum)
POTS (w/lids) - 2-Stainless Steel
FRY PAN - Stainless or Cast Iron
STEAMER - Stainless
BLENDER   COVERED BAKING DISH
COOKIE SHEET - Stainless

Basic Preparation Information

General Guide to Sprouting

Seed Type	Amount	Soaking Time	Growing Time	Yield
Sunflower	¼ cup	5 hours	10–15 days	½ cup
Alfalfa	¼ cup	5–6 hours	5–7 days	1 gallon
Mung	¼ cup	10–24 hours	3 days	¾–1 cup
Lentil	¼ cup	10–24 hours	3 days	¾–1 cup
Peas	¼ cup	10–24 hours	3 days	¾–1 cup
Cabbage	¼ cup	10–24 hours	3 days	¾–1 cup
Radish	¼ cup	10–24 hours	3 days	¾–1 cup
Fenugreek	⅓ cup	10–24 hours	3 days	1⅓ cups
Soy	1 cup	10–24 hours	3–4 days	4 cups
Kidney	1 cup	10–24 hours	3 days	4 cups
Garbanzo	1 cup	10–24 hours	3–4 days	4 cups

For most sprouts, place seeds or beans in jar. Cover with screen secured with a rubber band. Add at least four times the amount of water (the larger the bean, the more water is needed). After specified time drain and rinse. Let set upside down in a warm place (66-80 degrees) and cover the jar to keep it dark. Rinse the seeds twice a day until sprouts mature.

Sunflower seeds make an especially delicious addition to salads. Take uncracked whole seeds, soak them as usual, and watch them open. Keep them moist and let them grow into young seedlings about 3–5 inches long. Rinse off the old hull and serve fresh. They are extremely nutritious and have many wonderful uses.

Similarly, uncracked buckwheat can be sprouted to become buckwheat lettuce about 3–4 inches long.

Going with the Grain

Kinds of Grains

Brown Rice - Long and short grain, nutty flavor, particularly short grain. Unpolished. Versatile by itself, fried with vegetables, added to soups, stews, casseroles, covered with sauce, made into great puddings, used cooked in baked goods.

Buckwheat - Available whole groats and cracked fine. Sold in supermarkets as "Kasha", an old Russian and Jewish favorite. Great alone, with butter, a little salt, or cooked and mixed with sauteed onions and mushrooms. Nice for breakfast too. Hearty and very tasty.

Bulgur - Also known as bulgur wheat or cracked wheat. Delicate taste. Wheat berries that have been cracked, after steaming and drying. Nice with raw vegetables, cold in a salad, popular in the Middle East.

Millet - Light, mild flavor . . . a nice change in taste. Good as a breakfast cereal with butter or oil, sea salt or tamari, or sweet with milk, raisins, or nuts.

Whole Wheat Berries - Nutty, hearty texture. Tasty alone or mixed in with casseroles, stews, or topped with a sauce. A satisfying winter dish.

Oats - They come in four types - quick-cooking, steel-cut, whole groats, and rolled. Soothing, nourishing taste, can be cooked creamy or thick. A great old-fashioned cereal or used in cookies, quick breads, to thicken soups, baked fruit desserts.

Barley - Mild, nutty flavor. Very satisfying taste particularly in fall and winter meals. Great added to soups for a meal in itself, stews and casseroles.

Cornmeal - A real treat for breakfast sweetened with nuts and fruit and milk or salted with tamari and oil. Delicious plain with some butter.

How to Cook Grains

Brown Rice - 1 part brown rice to 2 parts water. Bring to a boil, cover, reduce heat to low, simmer 1 hour. Do not stir while cooking. Should be dry and each kernel identifiable, not mushy. It is also nice to add vegetable bouillion to water after it comes to a boil, using one bouillon cube per cup of water.

Sprouted Brown Rice - 3 cups sprouted brown rice to 2 cups water. We recommend using a cast iron pot. Cover pot and bring to a boil. Turn down to simmer for 30 minutes with lid on. Turn off heat. Keeping lid on, let sit for 15 minutes to complete cooking.

Buckwheat - 1 part buckwheat to 1½ parts water. Bring to a boil, cover, reduce heat, simmer for 10-15 minutes. Watch it cook: when the water has cooked through and the grain is dry and fluffy, it's ready. It can go fast and burn easily on the bottom so keep an eye on it. It does well if dry toasted in a pan first or with a tiny bit of oil to coat groats. For toasting we get best results if it is spread out in a frying pan rather than a deep pot.

Bulgur - 1 part bulgur to 1½ parts water. Bring to a boil, cover, put on low heat and simmer for 10-15 minutes.

Millet - 1 part millet to 2½ parts water. Bring to a boil, cover, reduce heat, cook on low heat for about 20 minutes.

Whole Wheat Berries - 1 part whole wheat to 3 parts water. Bring to a boil, cover, reduce heat, simmer for about 2 hours. Add more water if it seems too dry. If too wet, drain water.

Oats - Steel-cut groats need soaking first before cooking. Soak for 1 hour, 1 part groats to 2 parts water. Bring to a boil, cover, put on low heat and simmer for approximately 30 minutes. For rolled or "quick" oats, water needs to be boiled first. Use 1 part oats to 1 part boiling water. Use up 2 parts boiling water if you want the consistency to be creamier. Cover, reduce heat, and simmer 5-10 minutes.

Barley - 1 part barley to 2 parts water. Bring to a boil, lower heat and simmer for about 45 minutes.

Cornmeal - Use 1 cup with 3 cups of water. Be sure to use cold water. Bring to a boil while stirring. Then turn down heat slightly and continue stirring. Stir constantly or it gets lumpy. Takes about 10-15 minutes depending on the different cornmeals used and on fine or coarse grain.

Wild Rice - 1 cup wild rice, well rinsed, to 2 cups water. Bring water to a boil; a black iron pot works best. Cover tightly, return to a boil, then turn heat down and simmer about one hour or until tender. Do not stir.

Additional Tips and Alternatives for Cooking Grains

Salt may be added to cooking water, about ¼ tsp. sea salt per cup of uncooked grain.

One cup of uncooked grain yields approximately 3-4 cups of cooked grain.

Another way to cook grains to ensure fluffiness and to enhance the flavor is to sautee the uncooked grains first like a pilaf and cook in a flavored stock.

Saute dry grains first in a light oil, approximately 1 Tbsp. per cup of grain. Use butter, ghee or better butter if you like. When hot, add boiling vegetable stock, or add a vegetable bouillion cube or instant stock powder to water and cover. Simmer the grain until usual time called for in chart above. Appropriate for rice, millet, buckwheat, bulgur.

Check on grains after the suggested cooking time. If you enjoy them softer, cook longer. Taste often, using your discrimination about doneness.

Sprouting multiplies the nutritional value of grains, and adds to the flavor. It also reduces calories and makes them easier to digest. Most grains with intact kernels can be sprouted. One of our favorites is rice, but these instructions can be applied to others including millet, kashi, and buckwheat.

How to sprout long or short grain rice.

1. Soak rice 8–9 hours.
2. Drain off water - rinse.
3. Sprout for 2–3 days by putting the soaked rice in a bucket with small holes on the bottom to drain, or in a glass jar with a screen on the mouth (keep the jar upside down so it will drain).
4. Rinse the rice 3–4 times per day, then keep it in a warm but not hot place (60–70 degrees).
5. When you see small sprout tails growing from the rice, then it is ready to be cooked.

Use as soon as possible after sprouting (within 3 days). Rice gets bitter if it is sprouted too long or if left too long after sprouting or cooking. Yields 6–8 servings.

General Guide to Cooking Beans

Dry Measure (1 cup)	Water	Cooking Time
Garbanzo beans	4 cups	4-5 hours
Kidney beans	3 cups	1½ hours
Lentils	3 cups	1 hour
Split peas	3 cups	1 hour
Pinto beans	3 cups	2½ hours
Red beans	3 cups	3 hours
Soy beans	4 cups	pressure cook 1 hour
Black-eyed peas	3 cups	1¼ hours maximum

PART I

Favorites from the Oasis Restaurant

BEVERAGES

Purifying

Health Building

Polari-Tea

Yield: 2 cups

Polari-Tea is known for its delicious flavor and healthful qualities. Herbalists say that FLAX functions as a tonic, soothing and cleansing the respiratory and digestive system; FENUGREEK purifies the blood and lymph system; LICORICE energizes and soothes the kidneys and lungs; and PEPPERMINT comforts the stomach and combines with FENNEL to improve digestion.

Mix together:

1 part fennel seed	**1 part licorice root**
1 part fenugreek seed	**2 parts flax seed**

Bring 2¼ cups water to a boil. Add 1 rounded Tbsp. of seed mixture to water, cover, turn off heat and let steep for 5 minutes.

Add ½ Tbsp. dried peppermint leaves and cover. Let steep for an additional 5 minutes.

Vitality Drink

Yield: 1 serving

Per Serving: Calories: 208, Protein: 1 gm., Fat: 14 gm., Carbohydrates: 21 gm.

Combine in a blender:

6 oz. fresh orange juice (apple juice may be substituted)	**1 inch chopped fresh ginger**
	1-2 cloves garlic (optional)
	cayenne to taste (optional)
1 Tbsp. cold pressed almond or olive oil	
1 Tbsp. fresh lemon juice	

Drink and follow with 2 or more cups of hot Polari-Tea (see recipe above). Wait 1-2 hours before eating solid foods.

Almond Nog

HEALTH BUILDING

Yield: 4 servings

Per Serving: Calories: 377, Protein: 6 gm., Fat: 15 gm., Carbohydrates: 24 gm.

Whiz in blender for 30 seconds:

3 cups almond milk   **1 tsp. almond extract**
¼ cup honey   **¼-½ tsp. nutmeg**

(See Almond Protein Drink page 23)
Add and blend until the cream lightly thickens:
¾ cup whipping cream

Garnish each serving with a sprinkle of nutmeg.

Green Drink

PURIFYING DIET

Yield: 6-7 cups

Per 1 Cup Serving: Calories: 75, Protein: 1 gm., Fat: 0 gm.,
Carbohydrates: 17 gm.

Blend (strain optional) and serve:

1 quart orange juice or   **½ bunch parsley**
   pineapple juice   **5 drops peppermint extract or 2**
2 cups water   **Tbsp. fresh peppermint leaves**
2 large comfrey leaves

Fruit Juice Smoothie

PURIFYING DIET

Yield: 2 cups

Per 1 Cup Serving: Calories: 227, Protein: 1 gm., Fat: 0 gm.,
Carbohydrates: 56 gm.

Blend and serve:

2 cups apple juice   **½ cup frozen blueberries**
1 banana   **¼ cup fresh pineapple juice**

Strawberry-Orange Freeze

PURIFYING

DIET

Yield: 3 cups

Per 1 Cup Serving: Calories: 82, Protein: 1 gm., Fat: 0 gm.,
       Carbohydrates: 19 gm.

Blend and serve:
2 cups orange juice   **½ cup ice**
½ cup strawberries

Coconut Milk

PURIFYING

DIET

Yield: 2½ cups

Per ½ Cup Serving: Calories: 55,Protein: 1 gm., Fat: 5 gm.,
       Carbohydrates: 2 gm.

Combine in a blender or food processor and blend very well:
3 cups water
1 cup shredded coconut, fresh or dried.

Pour through a strainer, then squeeze the pulp to remove all liquid.
Discard the pulp.

Almond Protein Drink

HEALTH

BUILDING

Yield: 4 cups

Per 1 Cup Serving: Calories: 384, Protein: 12 gm., Fat: 15 gm.,
       Carbohydrates: 16 gm.

Make almond milk by blending well in blender, then straining:
1 cup almonds   **4 cups water**

Add to almond milk:
½ cup protein powder   **½ tsp. vanilla**
¼ cup liquid lecithin   **2 Tbsp. honey or fructose**

Blend well and serve.

Cardamon Protein Drink (an East Indian Shake)

HEALTH BUILDING

Yield: 3 cups

*Per 1 Cup Serving: Calories: 151, Protein: 9 gm., Fat: 4 gm.,
Carbohydrates: 16 gm.*

Blend until light and frothy:

2 cups milk	**2 tsp. vanilla**
½-1 cup ice	**1 tsp. cardamon powder**
4 Tbsp. protein powder	**½ tsp. cinnamon**
2 Tbsp. fructose	**¼ tsp. nutmeg**

Protein Drink

HEALTH BUILDING

Yield: 3 cups

*Per 1 Cup Serving: Calories: 129, Protein: 7 gm., Fat: 4 gm.,
Carbohydrates: 12 gm.*

Combine in a blender:

2 cups milk	**1 Tbsp. fructose**
1 Tbsp. malt powder	**½-1 cup ice cubes**
1 Tbsp. protein powder	

Blend well and serve.

BREAKFAST

Gourmet Vegetarian

Breakfast Tofu

Yield: 6 servings

See photo, page 49.

Per Serving: Calories: 329, Protein: 23 gm., Fat: 19 gm., Carbohydrates: 9 gm.

Saute over medium heat until onions and garlic are translucent:

1 onion, diced	**3 cloves garlic, minced**
1 cup green peppers, diced	**2 Tbsp. almond oil, ghee (pg. 32)**
½ cup liquid aminos	**or butter**
2 lbs. tofu, cut into bite-size	**1 Tbsp. basil**
cubes	**1 tsp. sea salt**

Add and stir gently until well-heated:

1 cup tomatoes, diced	**2 Tbsp. fresh parsley,**
(optional)	**minced**

Just before serving sprinkle with:

2 cups Cheddar cheese, grated
black pepper to taste

Blended Breakfast Tofu

Yield: 6 servings

Per Serving: Calories: 276, Protein: 16 gm., Fat: 22 gm., Carbohydrates: 9 gm.

Blend in a food processor:

2 lb. tofu
⅓ cup liquid aminos
¼ cup almond oil, melted ghee (pg. 32) or butter

Saute until soft:

¾ cup diced onions
¾ cup sliced mushrooms
1 Tbsp. oil

Pour blended tofu over cooked vegetables. Fold into vegetables with spatula. Cook until golden brown, flipping one time.

Garnish with fresh chopped parsley.

Spinach Breakfast Tofu

Yield: 6 servings

Per Serving: Calories: 232, Protein: 16 gm., Fat: 13 gm., Carbohydrates: 8 gm.

Saute in a skillet:
1 cup onions, diced
1 cup mushrooms, sliced
2 Tbsp. oil

Add:
1½ lbs. tofu, cubed

Grill until very hot.

Add:
1 cup grated Swiss cheese
¾ cup spinach, steamed
3 Tbsp. nutritional yeast

Stir until well mixed. Salt and pepper to taste.

Crepes

GOURMET

VEGETARIAN

Yield: 10-12 crepes

Per Crepe: Calories: 135, Protein: 2 gm., Fat: 9 gm., Carbohydrates: 11 gm.

Blend:
    2 Tbsp. arrowroot
    ½ cup water

Add and continue to blend:

1 cup whole wheat pastry flour	**½ tsp. sea salt**
1 cup milk	**a pinch of lemon rind, grated**
2 Tbsp. almond oil, melted butter or ghee (pg. 32)	

Let stand at room temperature until you are ready to begin making the crepes. Cook on a lightly oiled grill or frying pan over medium high heat. Pour ¼ cup of batter in pan. Quickly spread the batter from the center outwards making it as thin as possible. Cook until bubbles pop open. Flip over gently and cook briefly until crepe slides easily.

Crepes may be served immediately, or cooled, stacked with wax paper between the slices, and frozen or refrigerated for future use. To serve refrigerated crepes, reheat for a minute or two on a grill or in a frying pan and fill with your favorite filling.

Filling ideas:
1. Cold marinated vegetables, such as asparagus and broccoli.
2. Creamed vegetable sauces (see following recipe for spinach crepes).
3. Cinnamon, fructose and butter.
4. Any fresh fruit with whipped cream, yogurt or ice cream and garnished with slivered almonds.

Spinach Crepes

GOURMET

VEGETARIAN

Yield: 4-6 servings

Per Crepe: Calories: 356, Protein: 9 gm., Fat: 21 gm., Carbohydrates: 21 gm.

Saute:

2 onions, sliced thin	**2 Tbsp. tamari**
2 cloves garlic, minced	**1 Tbsp. Vege-Sal**
3 Tbsp. ghee (pg. 32) or butter	**1 tsp. thyme**
2 Tbsp. parsley	

Add a mixture of:
1 lb. frozen spinach, thawed and drained well
3 cups sour cream
½ tsp. black pepper

Spoon this mixture onto each heated crepe, then fold the crepe over. Top with a spoonful of sour cream, a sprig of parsley and slivered almonds.

Serve immediately.

Honey Granola

GOURMET
VEGETARIAN

Yield: 18 cups

Per ½ Cup Serving: Calories: 413, Protein: 11 gm., Fat: 17 gm.,
Carbohydrates: 40 gm.

Preheat oven to 300°.

Mix together well:

8 cups rolled oats	**1 cup almond oil**
3 cups sunflower seeds	**1½ Tbsp. cinnamon**
3 cups shredded coconut	**1 Tbsp. vanilla**
2¼ cups cashews	**1½ tsp. nutmeg**
2¼ cups walnuts, chopped coarsely	**1½ tsp. sea salt**
1½ cups honey	

Spread out on cookie sheet and bake for 1½ to 2 hours. Stir
occasionally. Cool and store in a tightly sealed container.

Tofu French Toast

GOURMET
VEGETARIAN

Yield: about 15 slices

Per Slice: Calories: 83, Protein: 5 gm., Fat: 1 gm., Carbohydrates: 13 gm.

Blend together to a thick, creamy consistency:

1 lb. tofu	**1 tsp. nutmeg (optional)**
1 Tbsp. honey	**1 tsp. vanilla**
1 Tbsp. cinnamon	**water as needed**

Dip bread slices into batter and gently scrape off excess. Fry on a
seasoned, oiled, cast-iron pan or grill. Cook well on each side and
carefully turn only once.

CONDIMENTS & APPETIZERS

Purifying

Health Building

Gourmet Vegetarian

Ghee

Yield: 1¾ cups

Per Teaspoon: Calories: 34, Protein: 0 gm., Fat: 4 gm., Carbohydrates: 0 gm.

Melt over lowest heat:
   1 pound butter

Remove from stove, being careful not to disturb. Let sit for 30 minutes. Skim off the foamy top. Ladle out the clear yellow liquid. This is the ghee. The cloudy milk solids that sink to the bottom of the pan may be discarded.

Cashew Chutney

Yield: 3½ cups

Per Tablespoon: Calories: 30, Protein: 1 gm., Fat: 0 gm., Carbohydrates: 3 gm.

Blend in a food processor:
   1½ cups cashews, soaked
   1 cup soft pitted dates
   1 cup water
   ½ cup lemon juice
   ¼ cup fresh parsley, minced
   ¼ cup raisins, soaked

   ½ Tbsp. fresh ginger, peeled and finely chopped
   1 tsp. sea salt
   a pinch of cayenne
   fresh mint to taste

Adjust spices to taste.

Pineapple Chutney

HEALTH

BUILDING

Yield: 3-3½ cups

Per Tablespoon: Calories: 14, Protein: 0 gm., Fat: 0 gm., Carbohydrates: 3 gm.

Cook for 20-25 minutes at low temperature, stirring occasionally:
2 cups diced pineapple	**¼ tsp. ground cinnamon**
¼ cup raisins and/or coconut	**¼ tsp. ground nutmeg**
¼ cup honey	**a pinch of cloves, ground**
¼ tsp. ground coriander	**a pinch of tumeric, ground**
	a pinch of cumin, ground

Cool to room temperature and add:
1 Tbsp. almond oil
½ tsp. liquid lecithin
a pinch of cayenne

Raw Chutney: Combine all ingredients and blend thoroughly.

Apple Date Chutney

PURIFYING

DIET

Yield: 6½ cups

Per Tablespoon: Calories: 11 , Protein: 0 gm., Fat: 0 gm., Carbohydrates: 3 gm.

Cook on medium heat until apples are soft:
2½ cup apples, diced	**¼ cup lemon juice**
6 Tbsp. raisins	**¼ tsp. garlic**
6 Tbsp. honey	**½ tsp. ginger juice**
4 Tbsp. dates, chopped	**¼ tsp. cinnamon powder**
½ cup orange juice	

Add and cook a few more minutes:
2½ cups peaches, chopped
1¼ cups bananas, mashed

Cool. Store in the refrigerator.

Acorn Squash Chutney

HEALTH
BUILDING

Yield: 3½ cups (6-8 servings)
See photo page 50.

Per Serving: Calories: 337, Protein: 5 gm., Fat: 18 gm., Carbohydrates: 31 gm.

Cut up into chunks and steam until tender:
3 medium acorn squash

Cool. Scoop out enough pulp to make 2½ cups and blend in food processor until creamy. Set aside.

Blend together in food processor until smooth:

1½ cups figs (remove stems)	**½ cup dates, pitted**
¾ cup soaked almonds (almonds that have been soaked overnight in water)	**½ cup almond oil**
	1½ Tbsp. fructose
	2¼ tsp. curry powder
	¼ tsp. cayenne (or less, to taste)

Add squash to the processor and blend until well mixed.

Curry Powder

HEALTH
BUILDING

Yield: ¾ cup

Mix together:

3 Tbsp. coriander, ground	**1 tsp. red chili seeds**
2 Tbsp. ginger root powder	**1 tsp. nutmeg, ground**
2 Tbsp. tumeric powder	**¾ tsp. asofetida (Indian herb)**
2 Tbsp. mace, ground	**¼ tsp. cayenne powder**
1 Tbsp. cardamom, ground	**¼ tsp. cinnamon, ground**
¼ tsp. fennel, ground	**¼ tsp. cloves, ground**
1 Tbsp. cumin, ground	

Store in air tight container.

Garam Masala Blend

Yield: ¾ cup

Mix together:

3 Tbsp. coriander, ground	1 tsp. nutmeg, ground
2 Tbsp. ginger root powder	¾ tsp. asefotida, powder
2 Tbsp. tumeric powder	(optional)
2 Tbsp. mace, ground	¼ tsp. fennel, ground
1 Tbsp. cumin, ground	¼ tsp. cayenne
1 Tbsp. cardamom, ground	¼ tsp. cinnamon, ground
1 tsp. red chili seeds	¼ tsp. cloves, ground

Store in an airtight container, in dark place. Use this blend to flavor masala dhosa rolls, rice, soups, and your favorite Indian recipes.

Better Butter

Yield: 3 cups

Per Teaspoon: Calories: 35, Protein: 0 gm., Fat: 3 gm., Carbohydrates: 0 gm.

Whip in blender or food processor until white and fluffy:
1 cup butter at room temperature

Gradually add while processor is on:
1 cup almond oil

Fold in:
1 cup lecithin spread

Ginger Juice Concentrate

Yield: ½ cup

Blend:
    ¼ cup ginger root, chopped
    ½ cup water

Strain well. Refrigerate for use in *Purifying* recipes like **Vitality Drink** (page 21).

Ketchup

Yield: 5 cups

Per Tablespoon: Calories: 35, Protein: 0 gm., Fat: 3 gm., Carbohydrates: 27 gm.

Cook until soft:
    4 cups tomato wedges
    1 cup water

Blend cooked tomatoes and the following ingredients in a food processor until smooth:

2 cups tomato paste (salt free)	**1 Tbsp. kelp**
	2 tsp. mustard powder
1 cup almond oil	**1 tsp. oregano**
½ cup molasses	**1 tsp. garlic granules**
1 Tbsp. basil	

Leftover ketchup can be frozen for future use.

Guacamole

HEALTH
BUILDING

Yield: 3½ cups (6 servings)

Per Serving: Calories: 340, Protein: 5 gm., Fat: 9 gm., Carbohydrates: 19 gm.

Mix together thoroughly:

3 cups mashed avocado
(about 6 avocados)
2 tomatoes, diced
½ cup diced celery
¼ cup red onion, diced
2 Tbsp. minced parsley

1-2 Tbsp. lemon juice (to taste)
2 cloves garlic, minced
½ tsp. chili blend
sea salt to taste

Serve with your favorite Mexican dish or as a filling for stuffed tomatoes. This guacamole makes an excellent sandwich spread or a filling for nori rolls.

Onion Dip

HEALTH
BUILDING

Yield: 2½ cups

Per Tablespoon: Calories: 35, Protein: 1 gm., Fat: 2 gm., Carbohydrates: 2 gm.

Saute for three minutes:

¼ cup dried onion flakes
3 Tbsp. liquid aminos (diluted)
1 Tbsp. tamari

Stir this into:

2½ cups sour cream
½ tsp. vegie salt
¾ tsp. fructose

Chill before serving.

Sweet Dip

Yield: *About 2 cups*

Per Tablespoon: *Calories: 48, Protein: 1 gm., Fat: 2 gm., Carbohydrates: 5 gm.*

Soak overnight:
½ cup almonds
3 dried apricot halves
3 dried figs

Grind in food processor and place aside in a bowl:
¼ loaf Essene bread

Grind in food processor:
**soaked almonds, apricots   ¼-½ cup almond oil
and figs**
½ cup dates

Add fruit and oil blend to the ground bread and mix by hand. Serve with fruit sticks.

Seed Pate

Yield: *3 cups*

Per Tablespoon: *Calories: 65, Protein: 2 gm., Fat: 3 gm., Carbohydrates: 5 gm.*

Prepare in advance:
¾ loaf plain Essene Bread, crumbled
¾ cup sunflower seeds, soaked overnight
½ cup almonds, soaked overnight

Add:
¾ cup grated carrot	**½ cup green pepper, diced**
¾ cup celery, diced	**½ cup red onion, diced**
½-¾ cup almond oil	**1½ cloves of garlic, minced**

Take half of the mixture at a time and blend it in a food processor until it is a smooth pate consistency. Serve on Essene bread or use as a dip with vegetable sticks.

Miso Pate

Yield: 2 cups

Per Tablespoon: Calories: 38, Protein: 1 gm., Fat: 5 gm., Carbohydrates: 2 gm.

Blend in a food processor until smooth:

2 cups small size bread cubes, toasted (2-3 slices)
2 cups celery, finely chopped
½ cup water or vegetarian soup stock
½ cup raw tahini
¼ cup fresh parsley, minced

¼ cup red onion, minced
3½ Tbsp. miso, white or yellow
2 small cloves garlic, pressed
½ tsp. sage, ground
½ tsp. rosemary, ground
½ tsp. thyme

Let the mixture sit overnight so the flavors blend. Spread pate on crackers or use it to stuff celery sticks to serve as an appetizer.

Yellow Rice Mix

Yield: 3 cups

Per ½ Cup Serving: Calories: 816, Protein: 1 gm., Fat: 61 gm., Carbohydrates: 0 gm.

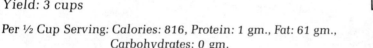

Melt:

3 cups ghee (pg. 32)

Add and saute on medium heat about 3 minutes, stirring constantly until mustard seeds pop:

4 Tbsp. curry powder - homemade recipe (pg. 34)
1 Tbsp. brown mustard seeds
1 Tbsp. cumin seeds
1 Tbsp. ginger root, grated finely

1¼ tsp. sea salt
1 tsp. tumeric powder
½ tsp. asefotida powder-optional (available at Indian spice stores)
¼ tsp. cayenne

Refrigerate. Cut off and melt as you need it. Can be used for masala dosa rolls and for seasoning rice.

Cheddar Cheese Pennies

GOURMET

VEGETARIAN

Yield: 2 dozen

Per Penny: Calories: 44, Protein: 2 gm., Fat: 1 gm., Carbohydrates: 2 gm.

Pre-heat oven to 400°.

Combine:

1 cup Cheddar cheese, grated	**¼ cup soft butter**
½ cup whole wheat pastry flour	**½ tsp. dry mustard**

Mix well. Roll into 1 inch balls and place 1 inch apart on an ungreased oven tray. Bake for 8-10 minutes. Serve hot.

Chevda (an Indian Snack)

GOURMET

VEGETARIAN

Yield: 4 cups

Per ¼ Cup Serving: Calories: 51, Protein: 2 gm., Fat: 2 gm.,
Carbohydrates: 4 gm.

Saute lightly:

2 tbsp. almond oil or melted ghee (pg. 32)	**2 Tbsp. raisins**
⅓ cup peanuts, lightly roasted	**½ tsp. cumin powder**
⅓ cup pine nuts lightly roasted or cashews	**¼ tsp. chili powder**
⅓ cup coconut, shredded	**¼ tsp. red chili seeds**
	¼ tsp. tumeric
	⅛ tsp. sea salt or to taste

Stir into:
    3 cups crumbled rice cakes, popcorn or puffed rice

Serve as a snack.

SAUCES

Purifying

Health Building

Gourmet Vegetarian

Savory Sauce #1

GOURMET
VEGETARIAN

Yield: *3 cups*

Per Tablespoon: Calories: 68, Protein: 0 gm., Fat: 7 gm., Carbohydrates: 0 gm.

Blend together in a blender:

½ **cup water**	½ **Tbsp. liquid lecithin**
¼ **cup liquid aminos**	1¼ **tsp. fresh lemon juice**
3½ **Tbsp. toasted garbanzo**	¼ **tsp. basil**
flour*	¼ **tsp. dulse seaweed**
2 **Tbsp. raw almond butter**	**pinch of garlic granules**

*To toast garbanzo flour, place flour in a cast iron frying pan. Stir over medium-high heat until flour turns golden brown and has a roasted aroma.

While blender is running pour in slowly:
   1½ **cups almond oil**

Delicious on steamed vegetables, rice and potatoes.

Savory Sauce #2

HEALTH
BUILDING

Yield: *2½ cups*

Per Tablespoon: Calories: 100, Protein: 0 gm., Fat: 11 gm.,
Carbohydrates: 0 gm.

Blend in a food processor (for 1 minute until smooth consistency):

2 **cups almond oil**	¼ **tsp. Vege-Sal**™
¼ **cup liquid aminos**	¼ **tsp. basil**
¼ **cup nutritional yeast**	1 **clove garlic**
flakes	¾ **tsp. lemon juice**
¼ **tsp. powdered kelp**	

Then add while the blender is on:
   ½ **Tbsp. liquid lecithin**

Stop the blender and add:
   ½ **Tbsp. fresh or dry parsley flakes**

Again, blend at medium speed for 3 seconds. Refrigerate.

Sunny Sauce

PURIFYING
DIET

Yield: 2 cups

Per ¼ Cup: Calories: 109, Protein: 5 gm., Fat: 1 gm., Carbohydrates: 5 gm.

Blend in a food processor or blender:

1 cup soaked sunflower seeds	**1 small clove garlic, minced**
½ cup water	**1 tsp. fructose**
¼ cup lemon juice	**1 tsp. kelp**
½ stalk celery, chopped	**¼ tsp. mustard**
¼ onion, chopped	

Adjust flavors to taste. This is a versatile and nutritious sauce for use on salads, steamed vegetables and baked potatoes.

Variations: Try adding ¼ cucumber (chopped), ¼ green pepper (chopped), basil to taste, or fresh parsley.

Eggless Mayonnaise

HEALTH
BUILDING

Yield: 4 cups

Per Tablespoon: Calories: 64, Protein: 0 gm., Fat: 7 gm., Carbohydrates: 1 gm.

Blend together:

1 cup milk powder	**½ tsp. sea salt**
¾ cup water	**½ tsp. dry mustard**
6 Tbsp. apple cider vinegar	

Add slowly while blending:
2 cups almond oil

As it sits, it will thicken. Keeps about 5-6 days in the refrigerator.

Mushroom Garlic Sauce

PURIFYING

DIET

Yield: 2½ cups

Per ¼ Cup: Calories: 209, Protein: 1 gm., Fat: 18 gm., Carbohydrates: 2 gm.

Blend together:
¾ cup almond oil	2¼ tsp. liquid lecithin
¼ cup olive oil	½ tsp. basil
3 minced garlic cloves	½ tsp. kelp
1 Tbsp. minced parsley	

Saute in a small amount of water:
    ½ cup onion, diced
    3 cups mushrooms, sliced

Cool. Add to oil mixture and stir well.

Shitake Mushroom Sauce

GOURMET

VEGETARIAN

Yield: 2 cups

Per ¼ Cup: Calories: 29, Protein: 1 gm., Fat: 2 gm., Carbohydrates: 2 gm.

Soak overnight:
    ½ cup dry Shitake mushrooms in 2 cups water

Drain water and set aside. Cut off heads, slice thinly, and steam until soft. Discard stems.

Saute mushrooms together with:
    1 cup sliced fresh mushrooms   1 tsp. safflower oil
    2 tsp. toasted sesame oil

Stir in:
1½ cups mushroom soak- ing water	1 Tbsp. grated ginger root or 1 tsp. ginger powder
2 Tbsp. liquid aminos	1 clove garlic, minced

Bring to a boil and stir in a mixture of:
    2 tsp. cornstarch   2 Tbsp. water

Simmer a few minutes. Remove from heat.

Almond Cream Sauce

Yield: 2 cups

Per Tablespoon: Calories: 60, Protein: 1 gm., Fat: 4 gm., Carbohydrates: 1 gm.

Soak overnight:
   1 cup almonds

Next day saute in a little water:
   6 Tbsp. onions, diced
   1 small garlic clove, minced

Blend the almonds and saute mixture with:
   ½ cup coconut milk   **½ cup almond oil or**
   **   (pg. 23)**   **   light safflower oil**
   ½ Tbsp. honey   **1 tsp. lemon juice**

Serve with steamed vegetables.

Orange Almond Cream

Yield: 1½ cups

Per Tablespoon: Calories: 53, Protein: 1 gm., Fat: 4 gm., Carbohydrates: 2 gm.

Blend until creamy:
   ½ cup almonds (soaked   **6 Tbsp. almond oil**
   **   overnight)**   **1 Tbsp. honey**
   ¼ cup coconut milk   **¼ tsp. vanilla**
   **   (pg. 23)**
   ¼ cup orange juice

Serve with fruit or baked yams.

Tartar Sauce

Yield: 1⅓ cups

Per Tablespoon: Calories: 51, Protein: 0 gm., Fat: 5 gm., Carbohydrates: 1 gm.

Mix together:

1 cup eggless mayonnaise, Nasoya or dairy (pg. 45)	1 Tbsp. fructose
1 Tbsp. fresh parsley, minced	1 tsp. wet mustard
1 Tbsp. dill pickles, minced	1 tsp. green onion, minced
	1 tsp. dill weed

Chill.

Mild Mexican Salsa

Yield: 2¾ cups

Per Tablespoon: Calories: 2, Protein: 0 gm., Fat: 0 gm., Carbohydrates: 0 gm.

Combine in a bowl:

2 cups diced tomatoes	½ tsp. ground cumin
½ cup diced red pimentos	¼ tsp. garlic juice or 2 cloves garlic pressed
¼ cup diced green chilies	¼ tsp. oregano
1 Tbsp. minced parsley	¼ tsp. cayenne
1¾ tsp. sea salt	⅛ tsp. red chili seeds
1 tsp. apple cider vinegar	

Stir well and let sit for at least one hour for flavors to blend. Adjust flavors to taste.

Barbeque Sauce Marinade

Yield: 4¾ cups

Per ¼ Cup: Calories: 108, Protein: 1 gm., Fat: 12 gm., Carbohydrates: 2 gm.

Mix together:

2¾ cups ketchup	¾ cup liquid aminos
1 cup almond oil	¼ cup Dijon mustard

See **Tofu Links Prepared for Barbeque,** page 91.

Marinara Sauce

GOURMET
VEGETARIAN

Yield: 3¾ cups

Per ¼ Cup: Calories: 52, Protein: 1 gm., Fat: 1 gm., Carbohydrates: 6 gm.

Saute:

1 cup diced onions	3 Tbsp. olive oil
1 cup sliced mushrooms	½ Tbsp. garlic juice

Add:

3 cups tomato sauce	¼ Tbsp. basil
¼ cup red or pink varietal grape juice (optional)	¼ Tbsp. oregano
	⅜ tsp. tarragon
1 Tbsp. parsley	¼ tsp. sea salt
1 Tbsp. fructose	1 small bay leaf
½ Tbsp. chervil	⅛ tsp. thyme

Simmer 20 minutes over low heat. Remove bay leaf. Use this sauce to make Lasagna (pg. 76). Serve with spaghetti noodles or other dishes.

Barbeque Sauce

HEALTH
BUILDING

Yield: 2 cups

Per ¼ Cup: Calories: 129, Protein: 1 gm., Fat: 1 gm., Carbohydrates: 30 gm.

Combine in a saucepan:

1 cup ketchup	1 Tbsp. chili blend spices
1 cup molasses	1 tsp. liquid smoke
½ cup yellow mustard (wet)	1 dash Tabasco sauce
¼ cup hickory bits (optional)	

Simmer over low heat for 3 minutes. Stir frequently. Refrigerate to cool.

French Barbeque Sauce

HEALTH

BUILDING

Yield: 3 cups

Per Serving: Calories: 67, Protein: 1 gm., Fat: 0 gm., Carbohydrates: 18 gm.

Mix together:

1 cup ketchup	3 Tbsp. sea salt
¾ cup molasses	2 Tbsp. liquid aminos diluted with
¾ cup wet mustard	2 Tbsp. water
¼ cup chili powder	¾ Tbsp. garlic powder
¼ cup onion flakes	

Keep refrigerated. Use this sauce over tofu, tempeh, or tofu burgers for picnics.

Vegetable Marinade

PURIFYING

DIET

Yield: 1 cup

Per Tablespoon: Calories: 62, Protein: 0 gm., Fat: 1 gm., Carbohydrates: 1 gm.

Blend together in a blender or food processor:

½ cup lemon juice	3-4 cloves garlic
½ cup olive oil	½ tsp. oregano
1 tsp. basil	to taste: rosemary, thyme,
1 tsp. kelp	marjoram
1 tsp. honey	

Use to marinate steamed and chilled mushrooms, onions and zucchini for a delicious cold salad.

Breakfast Tofu (pg. 26), Photographer: Alan Parker, Art Director: Mark Allison, Food Stylist: Susan Straithairn

SOUPS

Purifying

Health Building

Gourmet Vegetarian

Curried Sprouted Lentils (pg. 91) and Acorn Squah Chutney (pg. 34),
Photographer: Alan Parker, Art Directors: Mark Allison and Jane Buck,
Food Stylist: Barbara Maynord

Cream of Mushroom Soup

GOURMET

VEGETARIAN

Yield: 6 servings

Per Serving: Calories: 133, Protein: 3 gm., Fat: 7 gm., Carbohydrates: 7 gm.

Make a roux with:
   ¼ cup ghee (pg. 32) or butter
   6 Tbsp. whole wheat flour

Cook and stir with a whisk until mixture bubbles. Continue to stir for 1 minute. Set aside.

Combine in a sauce pan:

¾ lb. mushrooms, sliced	**½ Tbsp. marjoram**
2 Tbsp. liquid aminos	**sea salt to taste**

Heat until mushrooms are tender. Gradually add the roux, stirring constantly with a whisk.

Before serving add:
   6 Tbsp. cream
   2 Tbsp. minced parsley

Greek Tofu Soup

GOURMET

VEGETARIAN

Yield: 6 servings

Per Serving: Calories: 34, Protein: 3 gm., Fat: 2 gm., Carbohydrates: 1 gm.

Combine and boil:

4¼ cups soup stock	**pinch of sage**
1½ Tbsp. minced parsley	**pinch of rosemary**
½ tsp. thyme	

Let simmer for 15 minutes.

Add:
   ½ lb. tofu, cut into strips
   1 tsp. liquid aminos
   1 tsp. ghee (pg. 32) or butter

Simmer for 15 minutes, then add:
   1 tsp. lemon juice

Potato Corn Chowder

Yield: 10 cups

Per 1 Cup Serving: Calories: 117, Protein: 3 gm., Fat: 4 gm.,
Carbohydrates: 15 gm.

Combine:

5 cups water
2 cups corn
¾ cup celery, sliced
¾ cup onion, diced
¾ cup potatoes, diced
2 Tbsp. liquid aminos

¾ tsp. basil
⅓ tsp. dill weed
⅓ tsp. thyme
⅓ tsp. black pepper
a pinch of tumeric

Cook until potatoes and onions are tender.

Cook and stir with a whisk until mixture bubbles:
4 Tbsp. melted butter
6 Tbsp. whole wheat pastry flour

Continue to whisk for one minute.

While soup is simmering, pour the roux into soup, whisking
constantly and cook for 2 minutes.

Stir in:
1 cup milk or cream
2 Tbsp. minced parsley
sea salt to taste

Split Pea Soup

HEALTH
BUILDING

Yield: 4 servings

Per Serving: Calories: 283, Protein: 19 gm., Fat: 1 gm., Carbohydrates: 52 gm.

Wash well and cook until tender:

2 cups split peas	**5 cups water**

Then add:

¾ cup onions, diced	**2½ Tbsp. liquid aminos**
⅓ cup carrot, diced	**1 tsp. sea salt**
¼ cup celery, sliced	**1 clove garlic, pressed**
¼ tsp. apple cider vinegar	**1 bay leaf**
¼ tsp. thyme	

Reduce heat and simmer in covered pot for 1 hour until thick, stirring occasionally. Remove the bay leaf.

Six Bean Soup

HEALTH
BUILDING

Yield: 7 servings

Per Serving: Calories: 103, Protein: 6 gm., Fat: 0 gm., Carbohydrates: 20 gm.

Cook in soup pot until tender:

¼ cup lima beans	**¼ cup kidney beans**
¼ cup great northern beans	**¼ cup pinto beans**
¼ cup garbanzo beans	**16 cups water**
¼ cup black-eyed peas	

Then add:

1 cup onions, diced	**½ cup green peppers, diced**
1 cup celery, diced	**⅜ cup liquid aminos**
1 cup carrots, diced	**¼ cup parsley, minced**
1 cup tomatoes, diced	**1 Tbsp. garlic juice**

Adjust water level, if necessary, and cook until vegetables are tender.

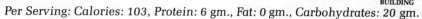

Minestrone Soup

Yield: 9 cups (8 servings)

Per Serving: Calories: 78, Protein: 4 gm., Fat: 0 gm., Carbohydrates: 17 gm.

In a large pot combine:

8 cups water	**1 tsp. oregano**
2 cups carrots, diced	**1¼ tsp. fresh basil**
1½ cups sprouted pinto	**1¼ tsp. marjoram**
beans or any other	**¼ tsp. garlic powder or 1 tsp**
sprouted bean	**garlic juice**
1¼ cups onions, diced	

Simmer over medium heat until beans are just soft, then add:

1½ cups fresh tomatoes,	**¾ cup corn kernels (salt free)**
chopped	**¾ cup green beans (salt free)**
1 cup zucchini, sliced	**sliced in 2 inch pieces**

Add and stir until mixed well:

¾ cup salt-free tomato paste

Simmer 5-10 minutes, stirring occasionally. Add more water if needed.

Tomato Soup

Yield: 4 servings

Per Serving: Calories: 167, Protein: 4 gm., Fat: 5 gm., Carbohydrates: 23 gm.

Make a roux with:

2 Tbsp. ghee (pg. 32) or butter
6 Tbsp. whole wheat pastry flour

Cook and stir with a whisk until it bubbles. Continue to stir for 1 minute.

Add:

5 cups water (whisking	**2 Tbsp. fresh parsley**
while adding)	**1½ Tbsp. fructose**
1¾ cups diced tomatoes	**1 tsp. dill weed**
½ cup tomato paste	**1 tsp. sea salt**
½ cup milk or cream	

Serve hot.

Sopa De Mexico

Yield: 6 servings

Per Serving: Calories: 228, Protein: 5 gm., Fat: 6 gm., Carbohydrates: 32 gm.

Combine in a soup pot and cook until tender:

8 cups water	**4 tsp. fructose**
2½ cups frozen corn	**4 tsp. chili blend**
1 cup green pepper, diced	**1 Tbsp. sea salt**
1 cup onions, diced	**2 tsp. ground cumin**
¾ cup tomato paste	**1½ tsp. ground coriander**
½ cup chopped green chilies (medium hotness)	**½ tsp. garlic juice or 1 or 2 cloves pressed garlic**
3 Tbsp. parsley, fresh minced	

Stir together in a small saucepan:
⅓ cup ghee (pg. 32) or butter
½ cup whole wheat pastry flour

Cook over medium heat and stir with a whisk until the mixture bubbles. Continue to cook and stir for one minute and then set aside.

Gradually add ghee-flour mixture to soup, stirring constantly with a whisk. Cook until thickened.

Black Bean Soup

Yield: 8 servings

Per Serving: Calories: 132, Protein: 8 gm., Fat: 0 gm., Carbohydrates: 25 gm.

Cook covered in a heavy pot until tender:
1¼ cups black beans
6 cups water

Then add:

2 cups water (approximately, to compensate for evaporation)	**2½ garlic cloves, finely minced**
	¼ tsp. thyme
1 small onion, chopped	**¾ tsp. basil**
	¾ tsp. oregano

¼ cup green chilies, chopped	1 small bay leaf
½ large green pepper, chopped	

Simmer until vegetables are cooked, then add:

¾ cup tomato paste	¼ cup finely-chopped Jalapeno peppers (optional)
1 tsp. vinegar	
sea salt to taste	

Heat to serving temperature. Remove bay leaf.

Smokey Lentil Soup

HEALTH
BUILDING

Yield: 6 servings

Per Serving: Calories: 94, Protein: 4 gm., Fat: 0 gm., Carbohydrates: 20 gm.

Wash well:
  1 cup lentils

Cook over medium heat for 30 minutes in:
  6 cups water

Add and cook for 15 minutes or until vegetables are tender:

¾ cup tomato paste	2 Tbsp. fructose
1 carrot, diced	1 tsp vinegar
½ onion, diced	½ tsp. garlic powder
1¼ stalks celery, sliced	½ tsp. basil
2 Tbsp. parsley, minced	⅛ tsp. liquid smoke
2 Tbsp. liquid aminos	sea salt (to taste)
	water (if needed)

Add water, if needed, to desired thickness and sea salt to taste.

Gazpacho

HEALTH
BUILDING

Yield: 8 cups (4 servings)
See photo page 150.

Per Serving: Calories: 194, Protein: 3 gm., Fat: 3 gm., Carbohydrates: 15 gm.

Liquify together:

3 cups tomatoes, chopped	**2 Tbsp. fresh lemon juice**
2 green onions, chopped	**2 Tbsp. paprika**
1 cucumber, medium	**½ Tbsp. sea salt**
¼ cup olive oil	**⅛ tsp. black pepper**
4 cloves garlic, pressed	

Stir in:

4 cups tomatoes, diced	**¼ cup red onions, minced**
1 cup unpeeled cucumbers, diced	**2 tsp. fresh parsley, minced**

Chill before serving.

Garnish with:
   4 sprigs parsley

French Onion Soup

GOURMET
VEGETARIAN

Yield: 7 servings

Per Serving: Calories: 148, Protein: 4 gm., Fat: 5 gm., Carbohydrates: 20 gm.

Saute in a medium sized pot until nicely browned:

5 onions, thinly sliced	**1 tsp. thyme**
¼ cup ghee (pg. 32) or butter	**1 clove garlic, minced or ¼ tsp. garlic powder**

Sprinkle over sauteed vegetables:
   ½ cup whole wheat pastry flour

Whisk in, whisking constantly, until flour is toasted.

Slowly whisk in:
   6 cups water
   ¾ cup liquid aminos
   ½ tsp. fructose

Bring to boiling point.

Garnish with:
⅛ cup fresh parsley, minced

Rich Vegetable Soup

GOURMET

VEGETARIAN

Yield: 5 servings

Per Serving: Calories: 137, Protein: 3 gm., Fat: 5 gm., Carbohydrates: 15 gm.

Simmer:

4 cups of water
1 carrot, diced
1 onion, diced
1 cup mushrooms, sliced
½ cup green beans, cut
3 Tbsp. liquid aminos
3 Tbsp. nutritional yeast

1½ Tbsp. minced parsley
½ tsp. Dijon mustard
½ tsp. sea salt
¼ tsp. each basil & tarragon
½ small clove garlic, pressed
pinch dill weed

Make a roux with:
¼ cup whole wheat pastry flour
3 Tbsp. ghee (pg. 32) or butter

Cook and stir with a whisk until mixture bubbles. Continue to stir for 1 minute. Add a little cool soup water to the roux to make a paste. Whisk the paste into the soup.

Simmer for 10 minutes.

Vegetable Chowder

Yield: 5 cups

Per 1 Cup Serving: Calories: 161, Protein: 3 gm., Fat: 8 gm.,
Carbohydrates: 13 gm.

Place in soup kettle and cook until tender:

5 cups water	**1 tsp. fructose**
½ cup onions, diced	**½ tsp. dill weed**
½ cup carrots, diced	**½ tsp. basil**
½ cup celery, sliced	**pinch of tarragon**
½ cup corn, frozen or fresh	**pinch of white pepper**
kernels	**pinch of black pepper**
½ tsp. sea salt	
4 tsp. liquid aminos	

Make a roux with:
    4 Tbsp. melted butter or oil
    6 Tbsp. whole wheat pastry flour

Cook and stir with a whisk until mixture bubbles. Continue to whisk
for one minute. Whisk into soup.

Add:
    ¼ cup cream
    1½ Tbsp. parsley, minced

Adjust sea salt to taste.

SALAD DRESSINGS & SALADS

SALAD DRESSINGS

Thousand Island Dressing

HEALTH
BUILDING

Yield: 2½ cups

Per Tablespoon: Calories: 39, Protein: 0 gm., Fat: 4 gm., Carbohydrates: 1 gm.

Blend together:

¾ **cup mayonnaise, soy or dairy (pg. 43)**	2 **tsp. molasses**
1½ **Tbsp. ketchup**	¾ **tsp. sea salt**
¾ **Tbsp. fructose**	½ **tsp. liquid aminos**
½ **Tbsp. apple cider vinegar**	½ **tsp. dry onion flakes**
½ **Tbsp. wet mustard**	½ **tsp. chili powder (mild)**
	⅜ **tsp. dry mustard**
	pinch of garlic powder

While blending pour in slowly:
   ½ **cup almond oil**

Turn off blender and stir in:
   ½ **cup dill pickles, minced**

Italian Dressing

HEALTH
BUILDING

Yield: 2½ cups

Per Tablespoon: Calories: 67, Protein: 0 gm., Fat: 6 gm., Carbohydrates: 1 gm.

Blend together:

1 **cup almond oil**	1 **Tbsp. marjoram**
½ **cup sour cream**	½ **Tbsp. basil**
¼ **cup apple cider vinegar**	¾ **tsp. fructose**
¼ **cup olive oil**	¾ **tsp. Vege-Sal™**
6 **Tbsp. lemon juice**	¾ **tsp. thyme**
¼ **medium yellow onion**	¾ **tsp. oregano**
4½ **cloves garlic, pressed**	¼ **tsp. black pepper**

Sour Cream Dill Dressing

Yield: 2½ cups

See photo page 149.

Per Tablespoon: Calories: 16, Protein: 1 gm., Fat: 1 gm., Carbohydrates: 0 gm.

Blend until smooth:

1 cup sour cream	½ tsp. Vege-Sal™
½ cup buttermilk	½ tsp. dill weed
½ cup cottage cheese	½ tsp. onion powder
2 Tbsp. scallion tops	¼ tsp. garlic powder
2 Tbsp. fresh parsley, chopped	¼ tsp. fructose
	pinch of pepper

Tofu-Miso Salad Dressing

Yield: 1½ cups

Per Tablespoon: Calories: 73, Protein: 1 gm., Fat: 7 gm., Carbohydrates: 1 gm.

Blend until smooth:

½ lb. tofu, crumbled	2 Tbsp. orange juice
¾ cup of oil	1½ Tbsp. brown miso
½ small onion	1 tsp. basil
1 small clove garlic	1 tsp. tamari
2 Tbsp. rice vinegar	

Bleu Cheese Dressing

Yield: 2½ cups

Per Tablespoon: Calories: 25, Protein: 1 gm., Fat: 1 gm., Carbohydrates: 1 gm.

Blend to desired texture:
- **¾ cup sour cream**
- **¾ cup cottage cheese**
- **⅔ cup bleu cheese**
- **½ cup buttermilk**
- **1 Tbsp. dried parsley**
- **½ tsp. sea salt**

Lemon Tahini Dressing

Yield: 1½ cups

Per Tablespoon: Calories: 45, Protein: 0 gm., Fat: 5 gm., Carbohydrates: 1 gm.

Blend until smooth:
- **½ cup tamari**
- **½ cup almond oil**
- **⅓ cup lemon juice**
- **¼ onion, chopped**
- **¼ green pepper, chopped**
- **¾ celery stick, chopped**
- **1½ Tbsp. water**

Sour Cream Onion Dressing

HEALTH

BUILDING

Yield: 2½ cups

Per Tablespoon: Calories: 32, Protein: 1 gm., Fat: 3 gm., Carbohydrates: 1 gm.

Blend until creamy:

1¼ cups sour cream	1 Tbsp. fresh parsley, chopped
10 Tbsp. mayonnaise (pg. 43)	½ Tbsp. dill weed
6 Tbsp. scallions or green onions, chopped	1 tsp. fructose
¼ cup lemon juice	¾ tsp. celery seed
¼ cup water	¾ tsp. Vege-Sal™
2 Tbsp. almond oil	

Sesame Dressing

GOURMET

VEGETARIAN

Yield: 2 cups

Per Tablespoon: Calories: 10, Protein: 0 gm., Fat: 0 gm., Carbohydrates: 1 gm.

Blend until smooth:

½ cup sesame oil	2 Tbsp. Parmesan cheese
½ cup almond or safflower oil	2 tsp. tamari
½ cup apple cider vinegar	½ tsp. dry mustard
½ cup lemon juice	honey to taste

Stir in by hand:
    ¼ cup sesame seeds, toasted*

*Spread on a cookie sheet and roast in a 450° oven for 5 minutes.

Herbed Oil Dressing

PURIFYING
DIET

Yield: ½ cup

Per Tablespoon: Calories: 90, Protein: 0 gm., Fat: 2 gm., Carbohydrates: 0 gm.

Blend until smooth:

6 Tbsp. olive oil	**¼ tsp. kelp**
2 Tbsp. lemon juice	**honey to taste**
1 clove garlic	

Optional spices (add to taste):

basil	**dill weed**
oregano	**tarragon**

Chili French Dressing

PURIFYING
DIET

Yield: 1½ cups

Per Tablespoon: Calories: 43, Protein: 0 gm., Fat: 5 gm., Carbohydrates: 1 gm.

Blend until smooth:

½ cup cold pressed almond oil	**2 Tbsp. chili spice blend**
¼ cup lemon juice	**1 Tbsp. fructose**
⅛ fresh medium sized tomato	**¼ tsp. dry mustard**
⅛ stalk celery	**¼ tsp. black pepper**
⅛ cucumber	**¼ tsp. paprika**
⅛ yellow onion	**¼ tsp. basil**
	¼ tsp. kelp

Summer Garden Dressing

Yield: 1¾ cup
See photo page 149.

Per Tablespoon: Calories: 41, Protein: 0 gm., Fat: 4 gm., Carbohydrates: 2 gm.

Blend until smooth:

¾ cup carrots, diced	1 Tbsp. fructose
½ cucumber, diced	2 tsp. honey
1 small onion, diced	¾ tsp. garlic granules
1 Tbsp. parsley, minced	¾ tsp basil
3 Tbsp. lemon juice	

Then pour in slowly and blend until smooth:
½–¾ cup almond oil

Ginger Tamari Dressing

Yield: 3 cups

Per Tablespoon: Calories: 28, Protein: 0 gm., Fat: 3 gm., Carbohydrates: 1 gm.

Blend well in a blender:

½ cup water	½ Tbsp. ginger, grated
1½ Tbsp. rice vinegar	3 Tbsp. red onion, minced
1½ Tbsp. honey	3 Tbsp. tamari
½ Tbsp. miso, yellow or white	1 garlic clove, minced

Pour in while blending at low speed:
½ cup almond or safflower oil

SALADS

Carrot Raisin Crunch

PURIFYING
DIET

Yield: 6 servings

Per Serving: Calories: 354, Protein: 7 gm., Fat: 8 gm., Carbohydrates: 47 gm.

Blend together for dressing, then set aside:

4½ Tbsp. orange juice	**1½ tsp. honey**
3 Tbsp. almond oil	**¾ tsp. cinnamon**
2½ Tbsp. lemon juice	**¾ tsp. kelp**
1½ tsp. olive oil	

Toss together:

4½ cups carrots, peeled and grated	**¾ cup raw sunflower seeds that have been soaked 4-8 hours in warm water and drained**
1¼ cups raisins that have been soaked 4-8 hours in apple juice and drained	**3 Tbsp. coconut flakes**

Toss the dressing into the salad. Garnish with fresh parsley sprigs.

Spinach Salad

PURIFYING
DIET

Yield: 6-8 servings

Per Serving: Calories: 368, Protein: 7 gm., Fat: 29 gm., Carbohydrates: 13 gm.

Toss lightly together in a bowl:

10 cups fresh whole spinach leaves, washed	**2 cups cucumbers, sliced**
2 cups cherry tomatoes, cut in halves	**1 cup red onions, sliced**
	½ cup raw sunflower seeds (soaked 4-8 hours in warm water & drained)

For dressing blend together until smooth:

¾ cup oil	**2 cloves garlic**
¼ cup fresh lemon juice	**½ tsp. kelp**

Optional Spices: basil, oregano, thyme to taste

Pour the dressing over the salad and toss lightly.

Mixed Sprout Salad

PURIFYING

DIET

Yield: 6 servings

Per Serving: Calories: 396, Protein: 6 gm., Fat: 36 gm., Carbohydrates: 16 gm.

Steam for 10 minutes:

1½ cups sprouted lentils   **1 cup sprouted mung beans**
1½ cups sprouted peas   **1 cup sprouted fenugreek seeds**
1 cup sprouted aduki beans

You may use other types of sprouts if you like.

Add to cooled sprout mixture:

1½ cups red onions, sliced
1 cup corn kernels (salt-free)

Blend together:

1 cup almond oil   **1½ tsp. kelp**
1½ Tbsp. ground chili   **1 tsp. curry powder, ground**
   blend   **½ tsp. cayenne pepper, ground**
**1 tsp. garlic juice or 4 medi-
   um cloves garlic, pressed**

Pour over sprouts and vegetables. Toss.

Garnish with:

½ cup fresh parsley, minced

Coleslaw

HEALTH
BUILDING

Yield: 8 cups

Per ½ Cup Serving: Calories: 87, Protein: 1 gm., Fat: 8 gm.,
Carbohydrates: 4 gm.

Mix together and set aside in the refrigerator for a few hours for
flavors to combine:

6 cups green cabbage,
sliced thin
1¼ cups grated carrots
1¼ cups eggless mayon-
naise
½ cup minced parsley
⅓ cup minced red onions

½ Tbsp. lemon juice
1 tsp. Vege-Sal™
1 tsp. pepper
⅔ tsp. apple cider vinegar
½ tsp. fructose

Papaya Jicama Salad

PURIFYING
DIET

Yield: 4 cups

Per ½ Cup Serving: Calories: 53, Protein: 1 gm., Fat: 0 gm.,
Carbohydrates: 13 gm.

Mix together in a serving bowl:
2½ cups papaya in ¾" cubes
2½ cups jicama in ¾" cubes
⅓ cup fresh lime juice

Sprinkle with:
paprika

Garnish with:
lime slices

German Potato Salad

GOURMET
VEGETARIAN

Yield: 5-6 servings

Per Serving: Calories: 261, Protein: 2 gm., Fat: 16 gm., Carbohydrates: 14 gm.

Mix and chill before serving:

5 cups pre-steamed &
   cooled red potatoes
   (cubed 1")
1½ cups sliced celery
1 cup sliced black olives
¾ cup shredded carrots
½ cup minced pickles (dill)

⅛ cup lemon juice
¼ cup rice vinegar
6 Tbsp. almond oil
6 Tbsp. chopped small red onions
½ Tbsp. yellow mustard
½ tsp. sea salt
½ tsp. black pepper

Tofu Salad

HEALTH
BUILDING

Yield: 3 cups
See photo, page 150.

Per ½ Cup Serving: Calories: 243, Protein: 8 gm., Fat: 21 gm.,
                Carbohydrates: 7 gm.

Mix well:

1 lb. tofu, well drained and
   crumbled
1 carrot, shredded
½ red onion, finely
   chopped
¼ green pepper, finely
   chopped
1 dill pickle, chopped

1 Tbsp. wet mustard
1 Tbsp. fresh parsley, chopped
¾ - 1 cup mayonnaise (pg. 43)
1 small clove garlic, minced
1 stalk celery, chopped
½ tsp. sea salt

Adjust flavors to suit your taste. Great as a sandwich filling, served on a bed of greens, or in a stuffed tomato.

ENTREES

Purifying

Health Building

GOURMET

VEGETARIAN

Gourmet Vegetarian

Murrieta Enchiladas

GOURMET

VEGETARIAN

Yield: 6 servings

Per Serving: Calories: 1037, Protein: 36 gm., Fat: 55 gm.,
Carbohydrates: 65 gm.

Preheat oven to 350°.

Have ready:
12 corn tortillas

To prepare **Enchilada Sauce**, bring to a boil:

6 cups water	**5 Tbsp. fructose**
4 cups diced onions	**1 Tbsp. ground cumin**
5 Tbsp. chili blend (mild)	**5½ tsp. apple cider vinegar**
5 Tbsp. sea salt	**6 cloves garlic, pressed**

Reduce to simmer until onions are cooked. Keep hot and set aside.

In another pan, whisk together:

½ cup almond oil	**½ cup melted ghee (pg. 32) or**
1 cup whole wheat pastry flour	**butter**

Bring to a boil. Whisk constantly for 2 minutes, then pour slowly into the sauce mixture, whisking until smooth. Set aside.

To prepare filling, in a separate pot steam until tender:
1 cup of diced onions

Cool.

Mix onions together with:
6 cups grated Cheddar cheese
2 Tbsp. sour cream

Dip each tortilla into sauce. Lay out and fill each tortilla with ½ cup of the onion-cheese filling. Roll up. Arrange in a 9" x 12" baking pan. Ladle remaining sauce over rolled tortillas. Cover and bake 40 minutes.

Garnish each serving with:
a spoonful of sour cream
sliced green onions
black olives

Spinach Quiche

GOURMET

VEGETARIAN

Yield: 10 cups

Per 1 Cup Serving: Calories: 254, Protein: 11 gm., Fat: 14 gm.,
Carbohydrates: 8 gm.

Preheat oven to 350°.

Mix together:
½ cup frozen spinach (thawed and water squeezed out)
½ cup Cheddar cheese, grated

Spread on the bottom of a pan or pre-made crust.

Blend in a food processor
¾ lb. or 1½ cups tofu

Then add and blend until smooth:

1½ cups cream cheese	**1 tsp. garlic powder**
¾ cup milk	**1 tsp. onion powder**
½ cup egg replacer	**½ tsp. curry blend**
1 tsp. sea salt	**¼ tsp. pepper**

Mix in by hand:
1 cup grated Cheddar cheese

Pour mixture into pan and top with:
2 Tbsp. Parmesan cheese

Bake 45 minutes.

Lasagne

GOURMET

VEGETARIAN

Yield: 12 servings

Per Serving: Calories: 742, Protein: 34 gm., Fat: 22 gm., Carbohydrates: 71 gm.

This delicious lasagne goes well with toasted garlic Parmesan bread, spinach salad with Italian dressing and a hearty burgandy grape juice.

For filling, mix together one at a time by hand until light and fluffy, then refrigerate:

1 lb. cream cheese	1 cup sour cream
3 cups cottage cheese	¼ cup butter, melted
1 cup Parmesan cheese, grated	a pinch of onion granules
	a pinch of garlic granules

For sauce, saute until onions are translucent:
⅓ cup olive oil
1 large onion, diced
4 cloves garlic, minced

Add:

4 cups tomato sauce	1½ Tbsp. basil
1 cup tomato paste	2 tsp. tarragon
1 cup water	1½ tsp. ground coriander
2 Tbsp. fructose	1½ tsp. sea salt
1 Tbsp. chervil	
1½ Tbsp. parsley	

Simmer on low for 20 minutes, stirring occasionally. Set aside.

For noodles, have ready:
2 lb. 3″ wide sesame lasagne noodles

Depending upon the type of noodle, cooking time will vary from 8-12 minutes. They should be prepared "al dente", which means cooked, yet still firm. While cooking stir occasionally so that all noodles are evenly cooked. You must watch and taste test during this time. A little oil added to the water helps prevent noodles from sticking. Drain in colander. Run cold water over noodles to stop cooking and facilitate handling. Drain well. You may cook noodles in advance and have them waiting.

Additional ingredients to have ready:
1½ cup Parmesan cheese, grated
½ lb. Provolone cheese, grated
½ lb. Mozzarella cheese, sliced ⅜″ thick

Assembly:
1. Preheat oven to 350°.
2. Place a light layer of sauce over entire bottom of 9" x 12" baking pan.
3. Place one layer of noodles over the sauce.
4. Divide the filling in half and place one half in little heaps like little cookie dough balls, evenly around the pan.
5. Sprinkle on ½ cup Parmesan cheese.
6. Layer ¼ lb. of Provolone and Mozzarella slices on top.
7. Repeat: sauce, noodles, filling, Parmesan, Provolone and Mozzarella.
8. Add one more thin layer of sauce and noodles. Then add a very light coating of sauce and sprinkle a light layer of Parmesan on top.
9. Bake for 25-30 minutes, or until golden brown, bubbly and the cheese is melted on top.
10. Remove lasagne from oven and let cool for 10-15 minutes. Cut and serve.

Chilean Zucchini

PURIFYING

DIET

Yield: 4 servings

Per Serving: Calories: 276, Protein: 12 gm., Fat: 2 gm., Carbohydrates: 33 gm.

Saute together until the onions are translucent:
1 onion, diced
2 ⅓ cups water

Add and cook for 8-10 minutes, stirring often to prevent sticking:

⅔ cup tomato paste	**¾ tsp. paprika**
½ Tbsp. chili blend spices	**¾ tsp. kelp**
2 tsp. fructose	**½ tsp. curry powder**

Add and cook for an additional 2-3 minutes:

3½ cups zucchini, sliced and lightly steamed	**¾ cups sunflower seeds, soaked 5 hours in water & then drained**
1½ cups tomatoes, medium chunks	**½ cup corn kernels (salt-free)**

Variation: Serve with 1¼ cups avocado chunks.

Tofu Rolls

Yield: 6 rolls

Per Roll: Calories: 447, Protein: 27 gm., Fat: 17 gm., Carbohydrates: 34 gm.

Preheat oven to 350°.

Have ready:

6 whole wheat chapatis	**1 lb. tofu, mashed**
4 cups Mozzarella, grated	**1 ½ cup tomatoes, diced**
1½ cups Marinara Sauce (pg. 47)	**¾ cup green pepper, diced**

To assemble rolls, lay out the chapatis and spread each evenly with the rest of the ingredients. Roll each up tightly and place in a 9" x 12" baking pan. Cover and bake for 35 minutes. Uncover and bake 5 minutes more. Best served right away.

Masala Dosa Rolls

Yield: 9 rolls

Per Roll: Calories: 399, Protein: 14 gm., Fat: 18 gm., Carbohydrates: 39 gm.

Steam until tender:
4 cups white baker potatoes, diced
1 cup white onion, diced

Grate:
2½ cups Jack cheese

Thaw under hot water to room temperature:
1 cup frozen green peas

Preheat oven to 350°.

Lay out on counter:
9 whole wheat chapatis

They can be grilled lightly on both sides in oil or ghee (pg. 32).

Melt:
½ cup yellow rice mix (pg. 39)

To assemble, stir together potatoes, onions, peas and yellow rice mix.

Spoon ½ cup of mixture onto each chapati. Sprinkle ⅓ cup Jack cheese over each chapati. Roll up. Place in 9" x 12" baking pan. Cover. Bake 30 minutes. Serve at once.

Cottage Rolls

Yield: 4 rolls

Per Roll: Calories: 242, Protein: 13 gm., Fat: 6 gm., Carbohydrates: 23 gm.

Preheat oven to 350°.

Have ready:
4 whole wheat chapatis

Lightly stir together:

1 cup Mozzarella cheese, grated	**⅓ cup cottage cheese**
½ cup tomatoes, diced– drain well	**¼ cup black olives, sliced - drain well**
	1 tsp. basil fresh or dried

Lay out chapatis on counter. Fill each chapati with ¼ of above mixture. Roll up and place in baking pan with lid on in oven for 30 minutes.

Before serving, sprinkle on top of each chapati:

2 Tbsp. Mozzarella cheese	**sprinkle of basil, minced**
2 Tbsp. tomatoes, chopped	

Serve immediately.

Quesadillas

Yield: 6 servings

Per Serving: Calories: 409, Protein: 19 gm., Fat: 17 gm., Carbohydrates: 29 gm.

Have ready:

6 whole wheat chapatis
1½ cups cheddar cheese, grated
1½ cups Jack cheese, grated

¾ cup black olives, sliced
¾ cup tomatoes, diced
¼ cup mild green chilies, diced
1 Tbsp. cilantro, minced (optional)

Saute slightly:

2 cups red onions, sliced   **1 Tbsp. almond oil or butter**

Lay the chapatis out on a counter. Divide and sprinkle all ingredients evenly on top of each. Pre-heat the grill or frying pan to medium heat.

Cook each quesadilla until cheese begins to bubble, then add to each:
4 thin slices of avocado

Fold in half and serve immediately.

Reuben Quiche

Yield: 5 cups

Per 1 Cup Serving: Calories: 471, Protein: 20 gm., Fat: 24 gm., Carbohydrates: 19 gm.

Preheat oven to 350°.

Blend in a food processor until creamy:
½ lb. firm tofu

Add and blend until creamy:
1½ cups cream cheese

Add and blend:

½ cup egg replacer
1 Tbsp. yellow mustard (wet)
1 Tbsp. parsley flakes

1 tsp. onion powder
½ tsp. garlic powder
½ tsp. sea salt

Then pour mixture into bowl, stir in:
2 cups sauerkraut, drained and squeezed
1½ cups Swiss cheese, grated

Pour into 9″ pie pan. Bake 50 minutes.

Garnish with:
5 tomato slices   **1 Tbsp. chopped green onions**

Swiss Spinach

GOURMET

VEGETARIAN

Yield: 6-8 servings

Per Serving: Calories: 458, Protein: 24 gm., Fat: 18 gm., Carbohydrates: 32 gm.

Preheat oven to 400°.

Lightly steam or saute in a little water:
2 lbs. mushrooms, sliced

Add:

3 cups frozen spinach,   **1⅓ cups cream**
**   thawed & squeezed**   **2 tsp. garlic, minced**
1⅓ cups Swiss cheese,   **2 tsp. sea salt**
**   grated**   **2 tsp. basil**
1⅓ cups Mozzarella, grated

Fold in:
4½ cups ribbon or macaroni noodles, cooked and drained.

Taste and adjust the spices as needed. Put in a 9″ x 12″ pan and bake for 1 hour.

Right after removing from the oven, top with:
⅔ cup Swiss cheese, grated   **⅔ cup Mozzarella cheese, grated**

Almond Creme Quiche

GOURMET

VEGETARIAN

Yield: 8 servings

Per Serving: Calories: 385, Protein: 17 gm., Fat: 18 gm., Carbohydrates: 20 gm.

Preheat oven to 375°.

Blend together:

¾ **lb. tofu**	1 **Tbsp. tamari**
½ **lb. softened cream cheese**	1 **tsp. dry mustard**
½ **cup water**	½ **tsp. sea salt**
4 **Tbsp. egg replacer**	¼ **tsp. nutmeg, ground**
2 **Tbsp. lemon juice**	⅛ **tsp. black pepper, ground**

Stir in:
   2 cups grated Swiss cheese

Set aside.

Chop, then set aside:
   1 lb. mushrooms   **1 cup green onions**

Layer green onions and mushrooms in the bottom of an unbaked whole wheat pastry shell (below) Pour cheese mixture over vegetables. Sprinkle with sliced blanched almonds. Bake for 45 minutes. Let sit for 10 minutes before serving. Garnish with fresh, minced parsley.

Almond Creme Quiche Crust

GOURMET

VEGETARIAN

Yield: 1 pastry shell

Per Shell: Calories: 910, Protein: 17 gm., Fat: 38 gm., Carbohydrates: 85 gm.

Combine in a bowl:
   1 cup whole wheat pastry   ¼ **tsp. sea salt**
      flour
   5 Tbsp. butter

Using a pastry cutter, cut butter into the flour until it is evenly distributed and the dough is pebble-sized.

Gradually add:

⅛ to ¼ cup cold water or orange juice

Dough will be firm. Handle dough as little as possible. Press into a pie pan, shaping a fluted edge. Fill and bake according to the directions above.

Savory Almond Quiche

GOURMET

VEGETARIAN

Yield: 6 servings

Per Serving: Calories: 596, Protein: 21 gm., Fat: 35 gm., Carbohydrates: 22 gm.

Preheat oven to 350°.

Blend in a food processor until creamy:
1 lb. tofu
1 8 oz. package cream cheese

Add and blend:

1 cup milk	**1 tsp. thyme**
1 cup bread crumbs	**1 tsp. sea salt**
¼ cup safflower or almond oil	**½ tsp. marjoram**
	¼ tsp. rosemary
7 tsp. garlic granules	**⅛ tsp. black pepper**

Pour this mixture into a bowl and stir in:
1 cup Jack cheese, grated
1 cup almonds, toasted and chopped

Bake in an oiled 9″ quiche pan for 40 minutes. Let sit for 10 minutes before cutting.

Tofu Yung

GOURMET

VEGETARIAN

Yield: 20 cakes

Per Cake: Calories: 47, Protein: 3 gm., Fat: 2 gm., Carbohydrates: 4 gm.

Blend in a food processor:

1 lb. or 2 cups tofu
⅓ cup water
¼ cup pastry flour
¼ cup egg replacer
2 Tbsp. tamari

1 Tbsp. toasted sesame oil
1" ginger root or 1 tsp. ginger
powder
1 clove garlic or 1 tsp. garlic
powder

Pour the mixture into a bowl and stir in:

1 cup crumbled tofu
½ cup sliced celery
½ cup grated carrots

½ cup sliced green onions
½ cup mung bean sprouts

Preheat grill or pan. Place ¼ cup mounds on oiled pan. Flatten. Turn when brown. Serve with **Shitake Mushroom Sauce** (pg. 44). Excellent cold for sandwiches. A great meal with a salad and toast.

Tofu Tidbits

GOURMET

VEGETARIAN

Yield: 3-4 servings

Per Serving: Calories: 519, Protein: 38 gm., Fat: 17 gm., Carbohydrates: 60 gm.

Preheat oven to 450°.

Cut into 1" bite size pieces:

2½ lbs. firm tofu

Mix together:

1¼ cups whole wheat flour
½ cup cornmeal flour
1½ tsp. thyme
1 tsp. garlic granules
½ tsp. onion powder

½ tsp. ground nutmeg
½ tsp. ground sage
½ tsp. tarragon
½ tsp. paprika
¼ tsp. rosemary, ground

Gently toss the tofu, one handful at a time, in the flour mixture until each piece is well coated. Place the tofu in a single layer on the bottom of a large baking pan. Bake until golden brown. Remove from oven and sprinkle with sea salt and pepper to taste.

Garnish with:
minced parsley

Serve with tartar sauce and lemon wedges.

Kabob & Tofu Marinade

GOURMET

VEGETARIAN

Yield: 10 Kabobs

Per Kabob: Calories: 324, Protein: 7 gm., Fat: 2 gm., Carbohydrates: 24 gm.

For marinade, mix together:

1 cup ketchup
1 cup liquid aminos
1 cup almond oil
1 cup water
1 cup pineapple juice
3 Tbsp. ginger juice

2 Tbsp. Tabasco Sauce
2 Tbsp. molasses
1 Tbsp. rice or apple cider vinegar
1 Tbsp. garlic juice

Marinate overnight:
20 1" cubes of firm tofu (1 lb.)
20 1" cubes of pre-steamed & cooled potatoes
20 wedges of red onion

Arrange on skewers with above marinated vegies plus:
20 cherry tomatoes,
20 1" squares diced green & red bell peppers
20 pineapple chunks.

Grill.

Chinese Tofuey

HEALTH

BUILDING

Yield: 8-10 cups (6-8 servings)

Per Serving: Calories: 170, Protein: 9 gm., Fat: 3 gm., Carbohydrates: 29 gm.

Preheat oven to 350°.

Toss together gently and spread out on a cookie sheet:
2 cups cubed firm tofu
3 Tbsp. liquid aminos

Bake 40 minutes—keep hot.

For sauce, combine in a saucepan and bring to a low boil:

3¾ cups water	**1 Tbsp. ginger juice or**
½ cup liquid aminos	**1½ Tbsp. ginger, finely grated**
1½ Tbsp. fructose	

Mix together, then whisk into the boiling mixture over medium heat:
7 Tbsp. cornstarch
½ cup cold water

Cook 2-5 minutes and keep hot.

Lightly steam until tender:

2½ cups carrots, sliced	**1½ cups cauliflower pieces**
2½ cups celery, sliced	**1¼ cups water chestnuts, sliced**

Add the last minute of steaming:
2 cups snow peas

Combine baked tofu, sauce and vegetables and serve right away.

Szechwan Tofu

Yield: 7 cups

*Per 1 Cup Serving: Calories: 141, Protein: 9 gm., Fat: 3 gm.,
Carbohydrates: 21 gm.*

Preheat oven to 350°.

Toss together gently:
1 lb. tofu, cut into 1" cubes
3 Tbsp. liquid aminos

Bake on a baking sheet 30 minutes.

For sauce, put in a saucepan and bring to a boil:

2½ cups water   **2 Tbsp. lime juice**
1-8 oz. can bamboo shoots,   **2 tsp. ginger juice (pg. 36)**
  drained   **2 tsp. garlic granules**
1-6 oz. can tomato paste   **¼ tsp. red chili seeds**

When boiling, whisk in a mixture of:
⅓ cup water
3 Tbsp. cornstarch

Cook, stirring constantly, until translucent and bubbly.

Steam for the amount of time indicated:

1 cup carrots, sliced diago-   **1 cup celery, sliced diagonally, 1**
  nally, 6 minutes   **minute**
2 cups snow peas, 1 minute   **¼ cup green pepper, diced, 1**
                                     minute

Combine all and serve at once.

Tofu Marinee au Champignons

GOURMET

VEGETARIAN

Yield: 6 servings

Per Serving: Calories: 393, Protein: 19 gm., Fat: 27 gm., Carbohydrates: 18 gm.

Mix together for marinade:

2½ cups water	1 tsp. paprika
¼ cup tamari	½ tsp. garlic
1 Tbsp. liquid aminos	½ tsp. ginger juice (pg. 36)
1 tsp. tumeric	

Cut into ¼" slices:
2 lbs. tofu

Place tofu in a pan and cover with marinade. Marinate overnight in the refrigerator. Drain and reserve marinade for sauce.

Saute:
1½ cups onions, diced
1 Tbsp. oil
4 cups mushrooms, sliced

Keep hot in a warm oven while frying all the drained tofu slices until they are golden brown. Keep them hot in the oven also.

Stir together in a saucepan:
the reserved marinade
⅓ cup cornstarch

Bring to a boil, whisking constantly until translucent.

Arrange half of the tofu slices and half of the onion mushroom mixture on the bottom of a serving pan.

Then sprinkle with:
1 cup Cheddar cheese, grated
half of the thickened marinade

Repeat and garnish with:
2 Tbsp. parsley, minced

Serve right away.

Tofu Nut Patties

Yield: 8 patties

Per Patty: Calories: 316, Protein: 10 gm., Fat: 19 gm., Carbohydrates: 19 gm.

Mix together:
> ½ **cup water**
> **1 Tbsp. egg replacer**

Pour into a food processor along with:

1 cup whole wheat bread crumbs	2 Tbsp. parsley
½ cup roasted almond butter	1 Tbsp. onion powder
½ cup walnuts, finely chopped	1 tsp. garlic powder
½ cup sunflower seeds, lightly roasted	1 tsp. thyme
½ cup millet or brown rice, precooked (pg. 16)	½ tsp. marjoram
2 Tbsp. almond oil	½ tsp. sea salt
	⅛ tsp. rosemary, ground

Process until well mixed, then stir in:
> **½ lb. tofu, crumbled**

Form into 8 patties. Place on grill or in frying pan and grill until browned on both sides.

Spinach Tofu Lasagne

GOURMET

VEGETARIAN

Yield: 6 servings

Per Serving: Calories: 530, Protein: 30 gm., Fat: 21 gm., Carbohydrates: 31 gm.

Preheat oven to 350°.

Cook al dente:
8 whole wheat sesame lasagne noodles

Rinse and cool. Cut into 9" lengths. Set aside.

Have ready:

2 cups Marinara Sauce (pg. 47)
1 10 oz. box frozen chopped spinach, thawed and squeezed dry

1 lb. tofu, crumbled and baked on a cookie sheet 30 minutes at 350°

To prepare filling, mix together lightly:

8 oz. cream cheese (crumbly variety)
1 cup Mozzarella cheese, grated
the baked crumbled tofu

⅓ cup Parmesan cheese, grated
1 tsp. basil
½ tsp. oregano

To assemble, spread ½ cup **Marinara Sauce** on the bottom of a 9" x 9" pan, then a layer of noodles, then another ½ cup **Marinara Sauce**. Next, spread half of the cheese filling, then half of the spinach. Begin again with a layer of noodles and repeat the sequence ending with a layer of **Marinara Sauce**.

Sprinkle on top:
1 cup Mozzarella cheese, grated
½ cup Parmesan cheese, grated

Bake 50 minutes covered and 10 minutes uncovered.

Curried Sprouted Lentils

HEALTH

BUILDING

Yield: 10 cups (6-8 servings)
See photo, page 50.

Per Serving: Calories: 211, Protein: 12 gm., Fat: 0 gm., Carbohydrates: 22 gm.

For sauce, bring to boil:

3 cups water	**1 tsp. garlic juice or 4 cloves**
2-3 Tbsp. honey (to taste)	**pressed garlic**
2½ tsp. ginger juice or 2	**1 tsp. ground cumin**
Tbsp. grated ginger	**1 tsp. sea salt**
2 tsp. curry powder	**½ tsp. cayenne**

Reduce heat and simmer while vegetables below are steamed.

Steam together:

8 cups sprouted red or	**1½ cups diced yams**
green lentils	**1¼ cups diced onions**
2 cups diced carrots	

Stir together sauce and vegetables. Adjust spices to taste. This dish is delicious served with coconut, raisins, green chilies, yogurt and whole wheat, oil-less, dairyless chapatis.

Tofu Links Prepared for Barbeque

GOURMET

VEGETARIAN

Yield: 6 servings

Per Serving: Calories: 455, Protein: 14 gm., Fat: 43 gm., Carbohydrates: 8 gm.

Choose enough firm tofu for approximately 2 to 3 slices per person. There are about 6 ½" slices per pound. Slice tofu into ½" slices and place in covered container and freeze overnight. Thaw completely. With palms of hands together, gently squeeze excess water from each tofu slice. Put tofu slices in a pan. Tofu is now ready to be covered with **Barbeque Sauce Marinade** (pg. 46), marinated overnight, and grilled.

Basic Seitan

Yield: 6 cups

Per Cup: Calories: 353, Protein: 39 gm., Fat: 2 gm., Carbohydrates: 44 gm.

Fluff gently together until the flour is completely dampened and the dough sticks together in a ball:
   4 cups instant gluten flour
   3¾ cups water mixed with
     ¼ cup tamari

Do not overmix or dough will be tough. Cut into four equal pieces and boil in a large pot 20-30 minutes or until cooked to center. Refrigerate to cool, then freeze if not to be used within three days.

French Dip Sandwiches

Yield: 6 sandwiches

Per Sandwich: Calories: 624, Protein: 24 gm., Fat: 31 gm.,
        Carbohydrates: 48 gm.

Have ready:
   3 cups French Onion Soup (pg. 58)
   3 cups seitan, cut into thin strips
   2 cups Barbeque Sauce (pg. 47)

Stir together seitan strips and barbeque sauce. Lift out the seitan strips and grill until well browned. Keep them hot.

Mix together:
   ¼ cup melted butter
   ¼ cup vegetable oil

Spread on:
   12 slices French bread

Grill until golden brown. Fill toasted bread with seitan strips to make 6 sandwiches and serve with a bowl of hot **French Onion Soup** for dipping. Serve right away.

Savory Wild Rice & Noodles

Yield: 5 cups

Per 1 Cup Serving: Calories: 349, Protein: 8 gm., Fat: 9 gm.,
Carbohydrates: 45 gm.

Have ready and keep hot:
   3 cups cooked long grain brown rice

Add to brown rice cooking water:
   ¼ cup liquid aminos
   3 Tbsp. dried onion flakes
   ¼ tsp. thyme
   pinch of sage
   pinch of rosemary
   ½ cup cooked wild rice
   ⅔ cup cooked spaghetti noodles,
      cut into ½″ lengths after cooking

Gently mix all together with:
   ⅔ cup pecans, chopped
   2 Tbsp. oil or melted butter (optional)
   1 Tbsp. parsley (minced)

Rice and Vegetable Nori Rolls

HEALTH

BUILDING

Yield: 5 uncut rolls

Per Roll: Calories: 95, Protein: 3 gm., Fat: 2 gm., Carbohydrates: 95 gm.

Mix well:

2 cups pre-cooked long grain brown rice or basmati rice	2 Tbsp. finely chopped fresh parsley
½ cup finely diced raw carrots	1 Tbsp. tamari (optional)
½ cup finely diced raw red onion	2 tsp. lemon juice
	1 tsp. dill weed

Have ready:
1 package pre-toasted nori seaweed
5 umeboshi plums, pitted (optional)

Take a sheet of nori and cover about ⅔rds of it with one-fifth of the rice mixture. Shred 1 umeboshi plum across the rice. Roll the nori and let sit for a while, until the juices have penetrated and softened the nori. Cut into one-inch slices with a very sharp knife.

Stuffed Artichokes

PURIFYING

DIET

Yield: 8 servings

Per Serving: Calories: 663, Protein: 18 gm., Fat: 33 gm., Carbohydrates: 45 gm.

Grind together in a food processor:

1 cup soaked almonds	½ cup fresh parsley, minced
1 cup soaked sunflower seeds	1 loaf of Essene bread
1 cup almond oil	6 cloves of garlic, minced
½ cup lemon juice	

Cut off the tops and steam until tender:
8 artichokes

Open the center and pull out a section about as big around as a quarter. Scrape out the hairs near the heart with a spoon. Fill with the mixture.

Garnish with:
A lemon twist
A sprig of parsley

Variation: Cut artichoke in half lengthwise. Scoop out the center, then fill and garnish as above.

Autumn Apple Bread Dressing

GOURMET

VEGETARIAN

Yield: 5 cups

Per ½ Cup Serving: Calories: 223, Protein: 5 gm., Fat: 8 gm.,
Carbohydrates: 28 gm.

Preheat oven to 350°.

Blend together and set aside:
¼ cup apple juice	**½ Tbsp. miso**
7 Tbsp. liquid aminos	**¼ tsp. garlic granules**

Saute together:
1½ cups onion, chopped
¼ cup safflower oil

Mix together in a large bowl:
2 cups whole wheat bread cubes	**3 Tbsp. parsley, minced**
	½ tsp. sage
2 cups long grain brown rice, cooked (pg. 16)	**½ tsp. thyme**
	½ tsp. sea salt
1 cup celery, sliced	**¼ tsp. rosemary**
½ cup pecans, chopped	**the sauteed onions**

Lightly mix in the wet ingredients. Place in a 1½ quart casserole or 9" x 9" pan and bake for 45 minutes.

Vegetable Pizza

PURIFYING

DIET

Yield: 8 servings

Per Serving: Calories: 305, Protein: 11 gm., Fat: 3 gm., Carbohydrates: 57 gm.

Preheat oven to 300°.

To prepare crust, spread in a thin layer on a 9" x 12" baking dish:
1 Tbsp. liquid lecithin

Blend in a food processor until smooth:

½ loaf Essene bread　　　**4 cloves pressed garlic or**
1 cup onion, diced　　　　　　**1 tsp. garlic juice**
1 Tbsp. liquid lecithin　　　**½ tsp. basil**
　　　　　　　　　　　　　　¼ tsp. oregano

Add just enough water to make blending easy. Pat crust into the bottom of the pan. Bake 45 minutes.

To prepare topping, blend together and set aside:

3 cups tomato paste　　　　**4 cloves pressed garlic or**
1 Tbsp. basil　　　　　　　　　**1 tsp. garlic juice**
2 tsp. oregano

Blend together corn layer and set aside:
5 cups corn kernels (salt-free)
1 tsp. onion powder

Have vegetables ready:
2 cups red onions, sliced in rings
2 cups green peppers, diced

Have toppings ready:

6 slices fresh tomato　　　**⅛ tsp. basil**
1 Tbsp. fresh minced　　　　**⅛ tsp. oregano**
**　parsley**

To assemble pizza, layer the tomato sauce on top of the baked crust. Spread the corn layer on top of the tomato sauce. Layer the vegetables on top. Sprinkle with basil and oregano. Bake for 30 minutes.

Before serving, top with:
the 6 slices of tomato

Sprinkle with:
the minced parsley

Soy Burgers

Yield: 8 burgers (4 servings)

Per Serving: Calories: 102, Protein: 7 gm., Fat: 1 gm., Carbohydrates: 10 gm.

Have ready and grind in a food processor:
2½ cups soybeans, sprouted and cooked well
¼ cup raw sunflower seeds (soaked 4-8 hours in warm water and drained)

Mix in:

⅔ cup onions, diced and pre-steamed until tender
⅔ cup carrots, grated
3 Tbsp. fresh parsley, minced
¼ tsp. ground kelp
1 small clove garlic, minced
¼ tsp. oregano

¼ cup water
¼ tsp. basil
⅛ tsp. ground sage
⅜ tsp. thyme
⅛ tsp. ground rosemary
pinch of cayenne

Form into 8 thin patties. Bake on ungreased cookie sheet at 400° until nicely brown.

Serve on sliced plain Essene bread with:

sliced onions
sliced tomatoes
lettuce

avocado
ketchup (pg. 36)

Use other unyeasted, oil-less breads for Health Building, or regular bread for Gourmet Vegetarian version.

Baked Harvest Vegetables

HEALTH
BUILDING

Yield: 6-8 servings

Per Serving: Calories: 229, Protein: 5 gm., Fat: 0 gm., Carbohydrates: 53 gm.

Preheat oven to 450°.

Place in a stainless steel or cast iron pot:

4 cups varietal non-sparkling white or pink grape juice
3 cups unpeeled yams cut into 1½" chunks
3 cups unpeeled carrots, cut into 1½" slices
3 cups unpeeled parsnips, cut into 1½" slices
3 cups peeled onions, cut into 1½" wedges
2 cups water

Cover with a tight fitting lid and bake for 60 minutes.

Then add:
3 cups celery, cut into 1½" slices

Continue baking for 30 minutes more. Remove from oven. Place pot on medium heat on stove and bring to a boil.

Mix together until smooth:
⅓ cup water
5 Tbsp. arrowroot

Pour into vegetable mixture, stirring constantly until it thickens and becomes clear. Remove from heat.

Garnish with:
¼ cup fresh parsley, minced

Facing Page
Lemon Coconut Dream (pg. 117) on Purifying Pie Crust (pg. 112), Photographer: Alan Parker, Art Director: Mark Allison, Food Stylists: Alan Parker and Jane Buck

Following Page
Glazed Fruit Tart (pg. 110), Photographer: Steven Simpson, Food Stylists: Jane Buck and Barbara Maynord

DESSERTS

Purifying

Health Building

Gourmet Vegetarian

Friendship Cake

GOURMET

VEGETARIAN

Yield: 8 servings

Per Serving: Calories: 308, Protein: 4 gm., Fat: 14 gm., Carbohydrates: 43 gm.

Preheat oven to 375°.

Sift together:

1⅔ cups whole wheat
pastry flour
1 cup fructose

1 tsp. baking soda
½ tsp. sea salt

Combine together:
1 cup buttermilk or sour milk*
½ cup almond oil
2 tsp. vanilla

*To make sour milk, add 1 Tbsp. apple cider vinegar to 1 cup whole fresh milk.

Add dry ingredients to wet ingredients and whisk lightly. Spread in an oiled, floured 9″ cake pan and bake for 30 minutes. (Using baking paper in place of oil and flour makes the cake easier to remove with less likelihood of cracking.)

Carob Cake: Add ½ cup toasted carob powder to dry ingredients.

Orange Cake: Add 1 cup orange juice and 1 tsp. cider vinegar and omit milk.

Spice Cake: Add 1 tsp. each of ground cinnamon and nutmeg and ¼ tsp. ground cloves.

Lemon Cake: Add 4 Tbsp. grated lemon rind.

Raspberry Jelly Rolls

Yield: 2 rolls (6-8 servings)

Per Serving: Calories: 748, Protein: 7 gm., Fat: 32 gm., Carbohydrates: 85 gm.

Make **Friendship Cake** batter (opposite page). Pour batter into two 9″ x 12″ pans lined with baking papers. Bake 20 minutes. It is important that the cakes do not become dry, so do not overcook. Cool completely. Spread two sheets of plastic wrap (larger than the size of the cakes) on a counter. Gently lift the cakes out of their pans by lifting up the sides of the baking paper. Very carefully flip the cakes over onto the plastic wrap. Gently pull off the baking paper.

Spread a thin layer completely over top of cakes:
⅔ cup your favorite raspberry jam

Gently lift the plastic wrap on one 9″ side until the top edge of the cake begins to fall over on itself to form a roll. Use your hands to keep the roll tight. Keep lifting the plastic wrap and stop every 2″-3″ to tuck the cake tightly into the roll and to pull the plastic wrap out of the roll. Also, you will need to keep pushing the jam back into the roll as it tends to get pressed out.

Helpful Hint: have a friend help you roll the cake. Four hands next to each other works best to keep the roll tight and even.

Blend together, then strain:
2 Tbsp. grated beets
3 Tbsp. water

Stir beet juice into:
1 cup coconut flakes

Set aside.

Whip until stiff:
2 cups whipping cream   **½ Tbsp. vanilla**
¼ cup fructose

Frost each roll about ½″ thick, including ends. Generously sprinkle the colored coconut over whip cream frosting. Use a long spatula to carefully lift decorated jelly rolls onto a serving platter. Chill. Best served same day.

Carob Cake

GOURMET

VEGETARIAN

Yield: 12 servings

Per Serving: Calories: 643, Protein: 10 gm., Fat: 23 gm., Carbohydrates: 80 gm.

Preheat oven to 350°.

Cream together:

2 cups fructose	**1 cup carob powder, sifted**
1 cup ghee (pg. 32) or butter	**1½ Tbsp. vanilla**

Then add:
2 cups cold decaffeinated coffee

Combine in another bowl:
4 cups whole wheat pastry flour
2 tsp. baking soda
2 tsp. sea salt

Sift the dry ingredients into the wet ingredients, alternately adding:
2 cups milk

Pour into a 9" x 13" pan that has been greased and floured. Bake for 45 minutes or until cake is done and still moist on top.

Carob Chip Cake

GOURMET

VEGETARIAN

Yield: 12 servings

Per Serving: Calories: 761, Protein: 10 gm., Fat: 28 gm., Carbohydrates: 105 gm.

Preheat oven to 375°.

Cream together:

1 cup fructose	**4 tsp. egg replacer mixed with ½**
⅔ cup ghee (pg. 32) or butter	**cup water**
2 tsp. vanilla	

In another bowl, combine:

2½ cups whole wheat pastry flour	**1 tsp. baking powder**
1 tsp. baking soda	**½ tsp. sea salt**

Mix dry ingredients into wet ingredients, alternately adding:
2 cups buttermilk

Fold in:
1¼ cups carob chips
½ cup chopped walnuts (optional)

Pour into two greased and floured 8″ round cake pans. Bake for 25 minutes.

Cheesecake

GOURMET

VEGETARIAN

Yield: 12 servings

Per Serving: Calories: 605, Protein: 9 gm., Fat: 27 gm., Carbohydrates: 59 gm.

Preheat oven to 350°.

Mix in a food processor until creamy:

3 cups cream cheese	**¼ cup egg replacer**
1 cup fructose	**1 Tbsp. vanilla**
1 cup milk	

Pour into a **Graham Cracker Crumb Crust** (pg. 114) in a 10″ spring form pan. Bake for 30 minutes. While it is baking, prepare the next layers.

Whisk well or blend:

2 cups sour cream	**2 Tbsp. lemon juice**
3 Tbsp. fructose	**2 tsp. vanilla**

When the first layer has baked the required time, pour this mixture over the top and bake again for 10 more minutes. Cool and cover with optional **Blueberry Sauce** (pg. 107).

Refrigerate overnight before serving.

Cranberry Nut Bread

Yield: 1 loaf (16 slices)

Per Slice: Calories: 145, Protein: 3 gm., Fat: 3 gm., Carbohydrates: 2 gm.

Preheat oven to 350°.

Combine:

2 cups whole wheat pastry flour	**1 tsp. sea salt**
1 cup fructose	**½ tsp. baking soda**
1½ tsp. baking powder	

Cut in with a pastry cutter:
2 Tbsp. hardened ghee (pg. 32) or butter.

Mix:
1 Tbsp. orange peel, grated
1 Tbsp. water
1 tsp. egg replacer

Stir in:
¾ cup orange juice

Fold in:
1 cup cranberries, coarsely chopped
½ cup walnuts, chopped

Pour into a loaf pan that has been lightly oiled and floured. Bake for 60 minutes. Cool 15 minutes before cutting.

Zucchini Bread

GOURMET

VEGETARIAN

Yield: 2 loaves (16 slices)

Per Slice: Calories: 347, Protein: 4 gm., Fat: 16 gm., Carbohydrates: 47 gm.

Preheat oven to 350°.

Combine:

3 cups whole wheat pastry flour	**1 tsp. sea salt**
2½ cups fructose	**1 tsp. baking powder**
3 tsp. cinnamon	**1 tsp. baking soda**

Whisk together and stir into dry ingredients:

1 cup almond oil	**3 tsp. egg replacer**
6 Tbsp. water	**1 tsp. vanilla**

Mix until moistened. Then fold in:

2 cups grated zucchini	**½ cup chopped walnuts**

Mix lightly. Bake in oiled loaf pans for 1 hour.

Blueberry Sauce

HEALTH

BUILDING

Yield: 2 cups

Per ¼ Cup Serving: Calories: 52, Protein: 0 gm., Fat: 0 gm.,
Carbohydrates: 13 gm.

Place in a saucepan and cook over medium heat:
2 cups blueberries, fresh or frozen

In a separate bowl, mix well:

⅔ cup apple juice	**4 tsp. cornstarch**
3 Tbsp. maple syrup or fructose	

Add mixture to berries. Bring to a boil until sauce is clear and thick, whisking constantly.

Tapioca

Yield: 6-7 servings

Per Serving: Calories: 542, Protein: 16 gm., Fat: 14 gm., Carbohydrates: 73 gm.

Soak together for 1 hour:
- **1⅓ cups small tapioca pearls**
- **1⅓ cups milk**

Combine in a double boiler:

10 cups milk	**½ cup cream**
soaked tapioca pearls	**¼ tsp. sea salt**
⅔ cup fructose	

Bring to a boil, whisking often, and cook until the consistency is creamy and thick like pudding and the pearls are translucent.

When cooked, remove from heat and stir in:
- **1½ tsp. vanilla**

Serve warm or refrigerate until cool. Add your choice of ingredients and/or vegetable food colorings when tapicoa has cooled:

Carob Chip Mint Tapioca: Add ¾ cup carob chips, ½ tsp. spirulina powder and peppermint oil or flavoring to taste.

Pink Peppermint Tapioca: Add ½ tsp. beet root powder or beet juice, peppermint oil or flavoring to taste and ½ cup crushed mints (idea: candy canes made from honey or fructose).

Orange Cream Tapioca: Add orange oil or extract to taste, 1½ tsp. orange rind and 5 Tbsp. orange juice.

Coconut Dream Tapioca: Add ½ cup toasted coconut flakes, almond extract (optional) to taste.

Mocha Carob Pie

Yield: 12 servings

Per Serving: Calories: 664, Protein: 17 gm., Fat: 24 gm., Carbohydrates: 52 gm.

Blend well:

3 cups tofu	3 Tbsp. powdered coffee substitute
1 cup melted ghee (pg. 32)	(such as Pero)
or butter	2 Tbsp. toasted carob powder
½ cup fructose	1 Tbsp. vanilla
½ cup honey	¼ tsp. sea salt

Add a little water, if needed. Pour into **No-Bake Pie Crust** (pg. 113).

Sprinkle with:
  carob chips

Chill at least 3 hours before serving.

Coconut Cream Pie:
Omit coffee substitute and carob powder. Add 1 cup soaked and drained grated coconut. Blend all ingredients as above, then fold in 2 cups whipped cream. Pour into pie shell and sprinkle with 2 cups lightly toasted coconut. Chill as above.

Blueberry Tofu Pie

Yield: one quart deep dish 9" pie (8 servings)

Per Serving: Calories: 385, Protein: 9 gm., Fat: 15 gm., Carbohydrates: 48 gm.

Preheat oven to 350°.

Blend:

1½ lbs. tofu	¼ cup melted ghee (pg. 32) or
½ cup maple syrup or	butter
honey	2 Tbsp. lemon juice
¼ cup milk	2 tsp. vanilla

Pour into an **Almond Pie Crust** (pg. 114) and bake for 30-35 minutes until golden yellow on top. Cool and cover with **Blueberry Sauce** (pg. 107).

Ricotta Yogurt Pie

GOURMET

VEGETARIAN

Yield: 8-10 servings

Per Serving: Calories: 529, Protein: 12 gm., Fat: 28 gm., Carbohydrates: 34 gm.

Soak in a sauce pan:
   2 Tbsp. agar granules
   1 cup water

Turn on to medium heat. Bring to a boil, stirring often. Boil for 3 minutes, then set aside.

Whip:
   ½ cup of cream

Set aside.

Cream until smooth in a food processor:
2 cups low fat yogurt	**½–¾ cup fructose**
1 cup cream cheese	**3 Tbsp. fresh lemon juice**
1 cup low fat ricotta cheese	**1 tsp. vanilla**

Whisk this mixture into the agar mixture, 1 cup at a time. Then add the whipped cream, continuing to whisk. Pour into a pre-baked 9″ pie crust. Refrigerate. Delicious served with a fruit topping.

Glazed Fruit Tart

GOURMET

VEGETARIAN

Yield: 1 15″ pie (16 servings)
See photo page 100.

Per Serving: Calories: 233, Protein: 5 gm., Fat: 7 gm., Carbohydrates: 32 gm.

Have ready:
   1-16 oz. bottle of juice of your choice (coconut-pineapple is great)
   2 Tbsp. arrowroot
   Fruit Pie Crust (pg. 111)

Mix ½ cup of juice with arrowroot until smooth with no lumps. Pour mixture into a saucepan with the rest of the juice. Heat up and stir continuously since it can easily burn. Mixture will look cloudy, then crystal-like, and then will boil. Cook for 3 minutes. It should pour off your spoon in sheets—a little thicker than the consistency of honey. Set pan aside and let it cool for a few minutes.

Artistically arrange the following items or other colorful fresh fruit to cover the cooked pie crust:

12 apricot halves	**3 kiwis, sliced**
30 cherries, red and black	**2 oranges, sectioned**
30 strawberries	**8 soaked almonds**

Pour a thin layer of jell over it—just enough to barely cover the fruit. Refrigerate for at least 30 minutes. Tastes great with whipped cream on top when served.

Fruit Pie Crust

GOURMET

VEGETARIAN

Yield: 15" pizza pie pan (16 servings)

Per Serving: Calories: 176, Protein: 3 gm., Fat: 7 gm., Carbohydrates: 2 gm.

Preheat oven to 424°.

Mix until flakey:

3 cups whole wheat pastry flour	**¼ cup fructose**
	2½ Tbsp. cream
¾ cups ghee (pg. 32) or butter	**2 Tbsp. non-instant milk powder**

Pat into buttered pan. Bake for 5 to 10 minutes until golden brown.

Purifying Pie Crust

Yield: 1 deep dish 9″ crust

Per Serving: Calories: 259, Protein: 6 gm., Fat: 11 gm., Carbohydrates: 15 gm.

Soak overnight:
⅔ cup sunflower seeds
⅔ cup almonds
⅔ cup raisins

Drain and grind in a food processor together with:
⅔ cup coconut
¼ cup almond oil

Pat into place. Chill and fill.

Pastry Nut Crust

Yield: 1 deep dish 9″pie crust (8 servings)

Per Serving: Calories: 330, Protein: 5 gm., Fat: 19 gm., Carbohydrates: 20 gm.

Mix together:

1 cup whole wheat pastry flour
1 cup ground walnuts
⅓ cup fructose

¾ cup cold ghee (pg. 32) or butter
5 Tbsp. water

Press into a pie pan.

Raw Pie Crusts

Yield: 1 deep dish 9" pie crust (8 servings)

PURIFYING

DIET

HEALTH

BUILDING

Per Serving: Calories: 282,
Protein: 8 gm.,
Fat: 9 gm.,
Carbohydrates: 27 gm.

Per Serving: Calories: 209,
Protein: 3 gm.,
Fat: 4 gm.,
Carbohydrates: 18 gm.

Combine:
- ⅔ cup soaked sunflower seeds
- ⅔ cup soaked almonds
- ⅔ cup soaked raisins
- ⅔ cup dates
- ⅔ cup coconut (optional)

Combine:
- ⅔ cup soaked dried apricots
- ⅔ cup raisins
- ⅔ cup coconut
- ⅔ cup walnuts or almonds, finely chopped

Put all ingredients through a Champion Juicer or grind in a food processor with ¼ cup of almond oil. Place in a pie pan and pat in place. Chill and fill with filling.

No-Bake Pie Crust

GOURMET

VEGETARIAN

Yield: 1 deep dish 9" pie crust (8 servings)

Per Serving: Calories: 617, Protein: 12 gm., Fat: 14 gm., Carbohydrates: 60 gm.

Stir together:
- 4 cups ground almonds
- 2 cups fructose
- ¼ cup melted ghee (pg. 32) or butter

Press into a round pie pan.

Almond Pie Crust

GOURMET

VEGETARIAN

Yield: 1 deep dish 9″ pie crust (8 servings)

Per Serving: Calories: 13, Protein: 2 gm., Fat: 7 gm., Carbohydrates: 19 gm.

Preheat oven to 375°.

Grind in a food processor or blender until very fine:
1 cup almonds

Add:

1 cup whole wheat pastry flour	**2 Tbsp. almond oil**
¼ cup honey or fructose	**½–1 Tbsp. water (optional)**
¼ cup ghee (pg. 32), melted or butter	**¾ tsp. cinnamon, ground**
	¼ tsp. sea salt

Mix thoroughly and pat in a pie pan. Bake 10 minutes until just golden in color. Great with **Mocha Carob Pie** (pg. 109).

Graham Cracker Crust

GOURMET

VEGETARIAN

Yield: 1 10″ crust (8 servings)

Per Serving: Calories: 290, Protein: 3 gm., Fat: 12 gm., Carbohydrates: 37 gm.

Mix together:
2 cups graham cracker crumbs
½ cup ghee (pg. 32) or butter
¼ cup fructose

For cheesecake, press into 10″ spring form pan.

Creamy Vanilla Pudding

GOURMET

VEGETARIAN

Yield: 7 cups

Per 1 Cup Serving: Calories: 26, Protein: 7 gm., Fat: 8 gm.,
Carbohydrates: 32 gm.

Heat in a double boiler, stirring occasionally (about 20 minutes):
5 cups milk   **½ cup fructose**
¾ cup cream   **¼ tsp. sea salt**

In another bowl, combine until smooth:
½ cup cornstarch
½ cup milk

When cream mixture is near a boiling point, slowly pour cornstarch mixture into double boiler. Cook about 10 minutes, stirring occasionally. Pudding will thicken. Remove from heat.

Add:
2 Tbsp. vanilla

Pour into serving dishes. Let chill in refrigerator.

Baked Yam Pudding

PURIFYING

DIET

Yield: 2 servings

Per Serving: Calories: 545, Protein: 9 gm., Fat: 17 gm., Carbohydrates: 80 gm.

Have ready:
2 cups mashed, cooked yams

Add:
3 Tbsp. honey   **¼ tsp. nutmeg**
1½ tsp. cinnamon

Top each serving with:
¼ cup Almond Cream Sauce (pg. 45)

Strawberry Jell

PURIFYING

DIET

Yield: 12 cups

Per 1 Cup Serving: Calories: 182, Protein: 1 gm., Fat: 0 gm.,
Carbohydrates: 46 gm.

Soak for 5 minutes in a medium saucepan:
1 cup water
8 Tbsp. agar flakes

Stir in:
1 cup apple juice
¾ cup fructose

Heat to boiling, set aside and cool.

Blend together:

2 cups pineapple juice	**1 cup strawberries**
1 cup apple juice	**¾ cup lemon juice**

Stir into cooled agar mixture.

Arrange on the bottom of a 9″ x 13″ serving pan:
3 cups pear slices
2 cups strawberries, cut in half

Pour agar mixture over fruit.

Sprinkle on top of jell:
1 cup grapes, stems removed

Chill until firm.

Lemon Coconut Dream

PURIFYING

DIET

Yield: 12 servings
See photo, page 99.

Per Serving: Calories: 338, Protein: 4 gm., Fat: 8 gm., Carbohydrates: 48 gm.

Have ready in a 9" x 12" pan:
Purifying Pie Crust (pg. 112)

Combine in a pot and bring to a boil:
3 cups pineapple juice   1 cup cold water
1⅓ cups fructose

In another bowl, combine:
3 Tbsp. agar granules
1½ cups warm water

Let sit for 1 minute, then add to above boiling mixture. Turn heat down, and cook until agar flakes dissolve.

In a separate bowl, mix together:
½ cup arrowroot powder
1 cup cold water

Whisk this mixture into above agar mixture until it thickens, about 2 minutes. Remove from heat.

Prepare coconut milk by combining:
1 cup coconut flakes
3 cups water

Blend for 2 minutes. Strain out flakes and use liquid.

Then add:
the coconut milk   6 Tbsp. lemon juice
6 Tbsp. lemon rind

Pour into the pre-made pie crust and chill.

Garnish with:
sliced lemons   1 Tbsp. coconut

Blueberry-Orange Jell

PURIFYING
DIET

Yield: 5 cups

Per 1 Cup Serving: Calories: 131, Protein: 1 gm., Fat: 1 gm.,
Carbohydrates: 32 gm.

Soak together in a medium saucepan for 2 minutes:
1½ cups pineapple juice
1 Tbsp. agar granules or 5 Tbsp. flakes

Bring to a boil and boil for 3 minutes. Stir and remove from heat.

Stir in:
1⅓ cup orange juice   **½ tsp. vanilla**
2 Tbsp. fructose

Place in a 5 cup pan or mold:
1 cup strawberries or   **1 cup apples, chopped**
nectarines, sliced   **¾ cup blueberries**

Pour the agar mixture over and refrigerate until set.

Pineapple Jell

PURIFYING
DIET

Yield: 8 servings

Per Serving: Calories: 228, Protein: 2 gm., Fat: 1 gm., Carbohydrates: 46 gm.

Soak together in a medium saucepan for 5 minutes:
2 cups cold water   **10 Tbsp. agar flakes**
2 cups pineapple juice   **or 2 Tbsp. granules**

Bring to a boil over medium heat stirring every few minutes. Simmer
until flakes are dissolved. Remove from heat.

Add:
2 cups pineapple juice   **4 Tbsp. lemon juice**
1 cup fructose

Arrange on the bottom of a 9″ x 12″ pan or 8 cup mold:
1 cup pineapple chunks   **½ cup almonds**

Pour liquid mixture into the pan or mold and refrigerate until firm.

Avocado Lime Jell

Yield: 5 cups

Per 1 Cup Serving: Calories: 217, Protein: 1 gm., Fat: 2 gm.,
                Carbohydrates: 37 gm.

Soak together in a saucepan for 1 minute:
1 cup water   **¾ Tbsp. agar granules (2 Tbsp.**
¾ cup fructose   **flakes)**

Bring to a boil, stirring often, and boil for 3 minutes.

Blend in a blender for 1-2 minutes:
½ cup coconut flakes
1½ cups water

Strain and retain the liquid (this is coconut milk).

Whisk ½ cup of the coconut milk slowly into the agar mixture. Set
aside the rest of the milk.

Blend in a food processor until smooth:
1½ cups avocado   **½ cup lime juice or lemon juice**
½ cup coconut milk

Then pour in slowly while processing:
the agar-coconut milk mixture

Process until smooth.

Pour into a 8″ x 8″ pan or a 5 cup mold. Refrigerate.

Carob Chip Cookies

Yield: 3 dozen cookies

Per Cookie: Calories: 195, Protein: 3 gm., Fat: 8 gm., Carbohydrates: 24 gm.

Preheat oven to 350°.

Cream, then set aside:
1¾ cups fructose	**4 Tbsp. cream**
1¼ cups ghee (pg. 32) or butter	**2 tsp. vanilla**

Mix together in another bowl:
3½ cups whole wheat pastry flour	**¼ tsp. sea salt**
2 tsp. baking soda	

Combine wet ingredients and dry ingredients. Stir by hand until just mixed.

Add:
2 cups carob chips
1½ cups chopped walnuts (optional)

Form into cookies and place on lightly oiled cookie sheet. Bake for 10-15 minutes or until golden brown. Cool completely before removing from cookie sheet.

Chewy Rich Brownies

Yield: 12 brownies

Per Brownie: Calories: 330, Protein: 2 gm., Fat: 15 gm., Carbohydrates: 39 gm.

Preheat oven to 350°.

Melt in a sauce pan:
¾ cup ghee (pg. 32) or
    butter,
    or ¼ cup almond oil
        ¼ cup lecithin spread
        ¼ cup cream cheese

Add:

1½ cups fructose
¾ cup sifted toasted carob powder
2 tsp. vanilla

2 Tbsp. liquid lecithin or 1 Tbsp. lecithin spread

Mix well and set aside.

In another bowl, mix:

1 cup whole wheat pastry flour
1 cup chopped walnuts
¼ tsp. sea salt

Stir only until combined, then add the carob mixture. Pour into a 9" x 13" pan that has been oiled and floured. Bake for 30 minutes. Cool and cut into squares.

Coconut Macaroons

GOURMET

VEGETARIAN

Yield: 4 dozen cookies

Per Macaroon: Calories: 41, Protein: 1 gm., Fat: 2 gm., Carbohydrates: 5 gm.

Preheat oven to 350°.

Blend:

1½ cups dry milk
⅔ cup milk
½ cup honey

2 tsp. egg replacer
2 tsp. vanilla
2 tsp. cardamom (optional)

Stir in by hand:

3-4 cups shredded coconut

Let the batter sit for 10-20 minutes so coconut can absorb moisture. Spoon onto a lightly oiled cookie sheet and bake for 10 minutes, until they just start to turn brown.

Gingersnaps

GOURMET

VEGETARIAN

Yield: 5 dozen cookies

Per Cookie: Calories: 83, Protein: 1 gm., Fat: 5 gm., Carbohydrates: 12 gm.

Preheat oven at 350°.

Combine in a large bowl:

1 cup almond oil
¾ cup fructose
½ cup honey

¼ cup molasses
2 Tbsp. apple cider vinegar

In another bowl, combine:

4½ cups whole wheat
pastry flour
4 Tbsp. ginger root powder

1 Tbsp. baking soda
1 tsp. cinnamon, ground
a pinch of cloves

Combine both mixtures and spoon onto a lightly oiled cookie sheet. Bake for 15 minutes.

Orange Ice Freeze

PURIFYING

DIET

Yield: 6 servings

Per Serving: Calories: 313, Protein: 4 gm., Fat: 14 gm., Carbohydrates: 28 gm.

Soak overnight:

¾ cup almonds

Drain and blend very well in a blender or food processor with:

3½ cups water
½ cup soaked almonds

¼ cup coconut flakes

Strain and discard pulp, retaining liquid.

Add to the liquid:

1½ cups orange juice
½ cup fructose

½ Tbsp. vanilla

Set aside. Soak together for one minute in a small saucepan:

3 Tbsp. agar flakes
1 cup water

Boil until dissolved. Cool for one minute.

Pour the two mixes into the blender and add while blending:
⅓ cup almond oil

Pour into an 8″ x 8″ pan and freeze. Remove from freezer ½ hour before serving.

Garnish with:
orange slices   **the remaining soaked almonds**
fresh mint leaves

Strawberry Ice Cream

PURIFYING

DIET

Yield: 8 cups

Per 1 Cup Serving: Calories: 402, Protein: 4 gm., Fat: 22 gm.,
Carbohydrates: 33 gm.

Soak together for one minute in a medium saucepan:
1 Tbsp. agar flakes
2 cups water

Bring to a boil 1 minute. Cool 1 minute. Set aside.

Blend well in a blender and strain:
4 cups water
1 cup soaked almonds
½ cup coconut flakes

Add to the strained mixture and blend together:
3 cups strawberries   **1 Tbsp. vanilla**
1 cup fructose   **soaked agar mixture**

Add slowly while still blending:
⅔ cup almond oil

Pour into 9″ x 12″ serving dish. Place in freezer until almost solid.

Angel Sauce

Yield: 2 cups

Per Tablespoon: Calories: 21, Protein: 2 gm., Fat: 0 gm., Carbohydrates: 2 gm.

Blend in a food processor until very creamy:
1 pint homogenized cottage cheese
⅓ cup fructose
1 tsp. vanilla

You may add sifted carob powder, fruit, sour cream or spices for variety. This delicious sauce is surprisingly rich and creamy and makes a nice dip for fruit slices.

Carob Sauce

Yield: 4½ cups

Per Serving: Calories: 44, Protein: 0 gm., Fat: 2 gm., Carbohydrates: 6 gm.

Blend one at a time in order:

2 cups water   **¾ cup melted ghee (pg. 32) or**
1½ cups fructose   **butter**
1 cup toasted carob powder   **¼ cup roasted almond butter**
¾ cup milk powder   **1 Tbsp. vanilla**

Serve over ice cream or any sweet treats!

PART II

Spa Cusine:
Lo-Cal Dining at Its Best

A Few Words
About Weight Loss

Our "Fit 'N Trim" Program at Murrieta Hot Springs has been very successful over the years. The basic dietary principles behind this success are very simple: eat the correct amount of calories for your level of activity while maintaining a reasonable exercise program. Increase exercise and decrease calories to the degree which is right for you. The successful diet is likely to be vegetarian, high in fiber and nutrients, and low in fat. It is important to note that just reducing fats (watch for hidden fats—cheese, avocados, nuts, seeds, coconut, for example) can have a dramatic effect by itself. These foods are best used sparingly as accents to highlight a dish.

Exercise programs may be varied for each individual, but we generally recommend a conscious routine that is fun. Set goals that are easily attainable. If you have not been exercising, be cautious and gentle with yourself. Choose activities with minimal impact and stress. At Murrieta Hot Springs, we use water exercise and low impact dance aerobics as primary weight-loss exercise activities.

We encourage our dieters to drink plenty of liquids. Overweight conditions are often accompanied by toxicity. The effective weight loss program will have a purifying effect as well. Water, herb teas, and fruit juices are a significant part of any program, especially if you are exercising. Our herb blend "Polari-Tea" is especially good for promoting the elimination of toxicity. To give your body an occasional rest, try a "mini-fast" by replacing breakfast with tea or juice and eating lightly in the evening.

Finally, let your diet reflect the demands of your lifestyle. A physically active lifestyle requires extra carbohydrates and more liquids.

Other tips for effective dieting include:
- Eat with someone. Enjoy eating as a social experience.
- Eat what you enjoy. Keep the portions small.
- Emphasize the aesthetics of eating. A nice environment, good friends, and a beautiful presentation complement your dining.

- Take time for preparation and for eating. Don't eat standing up while cooking. Sit down and savor the meal. You will feel more satisfied.
- Digestion begins in the mouth. Chew well so you can enjoy what you eat.
- Plan a balanced diet.
- Check your favorite recipes. With some creativity and knowledge of substitutes you'll find great savings in calories with no loss of taste.
- Provide small, satisfying portions. Use fine quality produce and selected gourmet delicacies rather than just "diet food." "Fit 'N Trim" is a way of life that promotes balanced nourishment and contentment at mealtime as well as throughout the day.
- Redo your favorite recipes using these lower calorie substitutes:

cheese . . . . mozzarella or other lo-cal cheese
chips . . . . lo cal crackers
cottage cheese . . . . lowfat cottage cheese
cream cheese . . . . yogurt cheese
eggs . . . . egg replacer
jams and jellies . . . . . . unsweetened fruit conserves
mayonnaise . . . . tofu mayonnaise
milk . . . . lowfat or nonfat milk
oil . . . . partially replace with soupstock, juices or liquid aminos
roux . . . . cornstarch or vegetable puree
sour cream . . . . yogurt
whipped cream . . . . . . whipped evaporated skim milk

Stocking the Pantry for Low-Calorie Cooking

agar flakes or granules
artichoke hearts
berries, frozen, unsweetened
bran
breads:
  pocket bread
  chapatis
  corn tortilla
  Dimpflmeier 100% rye plus

whole wheat English muffins
Essene: sprouted wheat or rye
Oasis no salt
Oasis pizza crust
brown rice syrup
buttermilk
capers
carob powder (toasted)

(Continued on next page)

Stocking the Pantry for Lo-Cal Cooking, cont'd.

cheeses:
  bleu
  dry curd cottage cheese
  lowfat cottage cheese
  lowfat Swiss
  Mozzarella
  part skim ricotta
  lowfat Cheddar
  lowfat garlic and chive Jack
  lowfat jalapeno Jack
  lowfat Monterey Jack
coconut, unsweetened
cornstarch
crackers:
  crispy rice cakes
  brown rice snaps
  wasa crisp breads
currents
dates
egg replacer
falafel mix
spaghetti sauce, low cal
flax seeds
flavorings:
  almond
  maple
  vanilla
grape leaves
grains:
  barley
  brown rice
  kashi
  millet
green chilis
hearts of palm
herbs, fresh & dried
juices:
  varietal grape
  pineapple, unsweetened
  sparkling apple, unsweetened
  sparkling grape, unsweetened
  tomato
legumes:
  kidney beans
  lentils, red and brown
  pintos
  split peas

liquid aminos
milk:
  evaporated skim
  nonfat
  nonfat powder
miso:
  red
  mellow white
  light yellow
mustard:
  Dijon
  miso
mayonnaise, Nasoya
oils:
  unrefined safflower
  olive
  almond
  toasted sesame
pasta:
  sesame wheat
  soba (buckwheat)
  vegetable rotelli noodles
salsa
sauerkraut
seaweed:
  agar flakes or granules
  hiziki
  kombu
  nori
seeds:
  pinenuts (pignolia)
  pumpkin
  sesame (brown & black)
  sunflower
spices, assorted, including:
  Spike
  Vegit
  Vege-Sal
tahini
tamari
tempeh
tofu/tofu cheese
vinegars:
  apple cider
  red wine
  rice
yogurt, lowfat

Menu Planning
From the Fit 'N Trim Program

800 Calories Per Day — A Menu for Two Weeks

Note—Calories include grains and beans which are sprouted.

Breakfast is **Vitality Drink** and **Polari-Tea**—160 calories

Alternate Breakfast   *160 calories*

A. ¾ **cup lowfat yogurt**
Choice of one of these fresh fruits:

3 dates	**1½ figs**
3 prunes	**1½ plums**
⅔ pear	**¾ nectarine**
¾ apple	**1½ tangerines**
3 apricots	**¾ cup pineapple**
1½ kiwi	**1 small bunch grapes**
⅔ banana	**1⅓ cup strawberries**

B. ¾ **cup cooked cereal**
with 7 soaked almonds
or ½ cup nonfat milk
with 1 tsp. fructose

Alternate Lunch or Dinner   *315 calories*

Salad with 2 oz. lo-cal dressing
1 cup steamed vegetable and one of the following:
A. 1 cup brown rice   **B. 1 baked potato with 1 Tbsp. sour**
                                      cream and 2 tsp. savory sauce

C. ½ cup lowfat cottage cheese   **D. ⅔ cup spaghetti noodles**
Soup of the day - 100 calories   **⅓ cup spaghetti sauce**
of any   **1 Tbsp. Parmesan sauce**

Week One Fit 'N Trim Sample Menu

Lunch	Calories	Dinner	Calories
¾ cup Gazpacho with Celery Heart	45	Strawberry Radicchio Salad	60
Salad with 1 oz. Vinaigrette	37	¾ cup Split Pea Soup	75
Sprouted Bean Tostada	210	Squash Stuffed with Pearl Onions	175
with ¼ cup Vegimole		½ cup Quick Fruit Whip	40
⅓ cup Lime Jell	28	Total	350
Total	320		
⅔ cup Tomato Bisque	22	Optional Fast	
Salad with 1 oz. Bleu Cheese	58	1 cup Leek Corn Chowder	65
Dressing		Salad with 1 oz. Fresh Herb Dressing	37
½ cup Baby Carrots	36	Reuben Sandwich	205
with Orange Glaze		1 Snowball	16
Spinach Touffle	197	Total	323
1 Snowball	16		
Total	319		
Fruit Plate of your choice	300	¾ cup Tofu Noodle Soup	66
with ⅓ cup Angel Sauce		Salad with 1 oz. Ginger Tamari	41
or ½ cup lowfat yogurt		Dressing	
Eat melons first - wait 10 minutes		Snow Pea Salad	65
Total	300	Sweet & Sour Cabbage Roll (sprouted)	157
		with ¼ cup sauce	
		Total	329
1 cup Miso Hiziki Soup	40	⅔ cup Confetti Salad	53
Salad with 1 oz. Ginger Tamari	41	1 cup Garlic Soup	60
Dressing		Small Artichoke with 1 Tbsp. filling	43
1½ cups Chinese Vegetables	195	& ½ tsp. pine nuts	
with ½ cup sprouted Kashi		⅛ Millet Loaf	150
2 crackers	26	Salad with 1 oz. Lemon Vinaigrette	44
Total	302	Total	350
Optional Fast		1 cup Smokey Lentil Soup (sprouted)	60
Curried Vegetable Soup	39	Salad with 1 oz. Cucumber Dressing	40
Salad with 1 oz. Lemon Tahini	58	½ serving Eggplant Manicotti	97
Dressing		½ cup Savory Spaghetti Squash	72
Pocket Sandwiches	215	Country Biscuit	72
with Cucumber Sauce		Total	350
Dolmas	23		
Total	335		
Fruit Plate of your choice	300	⅔ serving Pasta Salad	67
with ⅓ cup Angel Sauce		¾ cup Barley Soup (sprouted)	48
or ½ cup lowfat yogurt		⅔ serving Cauliflower Bechamel	132
Eat melons first - wait 10 minutes		⅔ cup Peas & Pearl Onions	58
Total	300	Total	305
1 cup Missing Bean Salad	72	South of the Border Salad	42
Artichoke	43	Salad with 1 oz. Lime Dressing	36
Broccoli Pizza	157	Enchilada	200
Coffee Gelato	30	2 Tbsp. Bean Sauce	18
Total	322	2 Tbsp. Salsa Dip	22
		Total	318

Week Two Fit 'N Trim Sample Menu

Lunch	Calories	Dinner	Calories
⅔ cup Borscht	52	Wild Rice Salad with	89
Salad with 1 oz. Cucumber Dressing	34	1 oz. Savory Dressing	
⅓ cup Tofu Burger	190	Salad with 1 oz. Vinaigrette	33
with fixins on bun		Lemon Pepper Kabobs (1½)	108
Corn on the Cob	50	Baby Artichoke with	32
Total	326	2 Tbsp. sprouted Hummus	
		Cherry Cheesecake Squares	82
		Total	344
Optional Fast		½ cup Asparagus	34
Salad with 1 oz. Lime Dressing	36	with 2 Tbsp. Lemon Caper Sauce	
1 cup Murrieta Chili (sprouted)	165	Salad with 1 oz. Italian Dressing	53
8 Tortilla Chips	60	Zucchini Frittata	185
¼ cup Vegimole	42	with Mushroom Sauce	
2 Tbsp. Salsa Dip	21	¼ cup Beet Relish with rye cracker	56
Total	324	Total	328
Fruit Plate of your choice	300	1 cup Garlic Soup	60
with ⅓ cup Angel Sauce		Salad with 1 oz. Cucumber Dressing	35
or ½ cup lowfat yogurt		Spaghetti Balls	192
Eat melons first - wait 10 minutes		Pesto with cracker	44
Total	300	Total	331
Salad with 1 oz. Sesame Dressing	76	⅔ cup chilled Asparagus Soup	40
½ cup Cream of Asparagus Soup	30	Salad with 1 oz. Lemon	44
Stir Fry	186	Vinaigrette Dressing	
¼ cup Pineapple Coconut Jell	41	Rainy Day Stew & Country Biscuits	210
Total	303	Corn on the Cob	50
		Total	344
Optional Fast		¾ cup Creamy Carrot Soup	35
½ cup chilled Cucumber Soup	37	Potpourri Salad	35
Reuben Sandwich	205	Salad with ½ oz. Lo-Cal	38
⅔ cup Confetti Salad	53	Sesame Dressing	
3 oz. Orange Sorbet	47	Vegetable Crepe	189
Total	342	Butterscotch Brownie	53
		Total	350
Fruit Plate of your choice	300	1 cup French Onion Soup	81
with ⅓ cup Angel Sauce		¼ cup Carrot Crunch	42
or ½ cup lowfat yogurt		Salad with 1 oz. Italian Dressing	53
Eat melons first - wait 10 minutes		¼ cup Bean Dip with celery	39
Total	300	Vegetable Puff	108
		Total	323
1 cup Asparagus	49	1 cup Smokey Lentil Soup (sprouted)	60
with 1 Tbsp. Mustard Sauce		Salad with 1 oz. Vinaigrette	33
1 cup Miso Vegetable Soup	50	Mushrooms Stuffed with Wild Rice	108
Tofu Salad in Tomato Flower	161	¼ cup Ginger Mint Coleslaw	37
2 Crispy Cakes	40	Baby Squash with Orange Glaze	42
Carrot, celery & jicama sticks	20	Lemon Spice Cookie	53
Total	320	Total	333

BEVERAGES

Purifying

Spirulina Drink

Yield: 4 cups

Per Cup: Calories: 30, Protein: 0 gm., Fat: 0 gm., Carbohydrates: 8 gm.

Mix:
   3 cups water
   1 cup juice (apple or pineapple)
   ½ tsp. spirulina

Lo-Cal Vitality Drink

Yield: two servings

Per Serving: Calories: 160, Protein: 1 gm., Fat: 14 gm., Carbohydrates: 12 gm.

Blend together:

**4 Tbsp. grated ginger root
   (or 1 Tbsp. ginger juice
   pg. 36)
3 Tbsp. lemon juice**

**1 Tbsp. cold pressed oil (almond,
   olive or safflower)**

Add:
   2 ½ Tbsp. to 6 oz. fresh orange juice or apple juice

Cayenne and garlic may be added.

Sunset Spritzer

PURIFYING

DIET

Yield: 6 eight oz. glasses

Per Serving: Calories: 10, Protein: 1 gm., Fat: 0 gm., Carbohydrates: 19 gm.

Puree in a blender:
   ½ cup sliced peaches (fresh or frozen, unsweetened)
   ½ cup boysenberries (fresh or frozen, unsweetened)

Place puree in a fine strainer.

Pour through the strainer:
   1½ qts. (6 cups) chilled sparkling mineral water, lemon or lime flavored

Serve immediately.

CONDIMENTS & APPETIZERS

Health Building

Gourmet Vegetarian

Beet Relish

HEALTH
BUILDING

Yield: 4 cups

Per ½ Cup Serving: Calories: 42, Protein: 2 gm., Fat: 1 gm.,
Carbohydrates: 6 gm.

Mix together:

4 cups small diced cooked beets
1 cup lowfat yogurt
¼ cup red wine vinegar

¾ tsp. coarse black pepper
½ tsp. Vege-Sal™

Tofu Hummus

GOURMET

VEGETARIAN

Yield: 2 cups

Per Tablespoon: Calories: 16, Protein: 1 gm., Fat: 0 gm., Carbohydrates: 3 gm.

Blend in a food processor:
½ lb. tofu
1 cup cooked garbanzos
¼ cup fresh parsley
3 Tbsp. lemon juice
1 Tbsp. toasted ground sesame seeds
1 tsp. garlic powder
1 tsp. coriander
½ tsp. cumin
½ tsp. Vege-Sal™

Chill several hours before serving.

Bleu Cheese Dip

Yield: 3 cups

Per Tablespoon: Calories: 20, Protein: 2 gm., Fat: 1 gm., Carbohydrates: 1 gm.

Blend together:
1½ cups bleu cheese
1½ cups lowfat yogurt
1 cup tofu

Best if made a day ahead.

Bean Dip

Yield: 2½ cups

Per ¼ Cup Serving: Calories: 52, Protein: 3 gm., Fat: 0 gm.,
Carbohydrates: 8 gm.

Blend in a food processor:
2 cups cooked black beans
1 cup Salsa Verde (pg. 147)
1 tsp. Vege-Sal™

Pesto

Yield: 3 cups

Per Tablespoon: Calories: 12, Protein: 1 gm., Fat: 0 gm., Carbohydrates: 0 gm.

Combine in a food processor until smooth:
2 cups fresh basil leaves **2 Tbsp. olive oil**
2 cups spinach, thawed and **2 Tbsp. pine nuts**
**   drained (or 4 cups fresh)** **10 garlic cloves**
¼ cup Parmesan cheese

Country Biscuits

Yield: 1½ dozen

Per Biscuit: Calories: 70, Protein: 3 gm., Fat: 2 gm., Carbohydrates: 10 gm.

Preheat oven to 375°.

Combine:

1½ cups whole wheat flour	**¼ cup Parmesan cheese**
½ cup unbleached white flour	**1 Tbsp. baking powder**

Cut in:
¼ cup butter until lumps form

Add, stirring just to moisten:
1 cup buttermilk

Drop by tablespoon onto baking sheet. Bake for 15 minutes.

Herbed Country Biscuits: Substitute ¼ cup Spike Seasoning™ or other herb blend for Parmesan cheese.

Vegi-Mole

Yield: 3 cups

Per ¼ Cup Serving: Calories: 42, Protein: 1 gm., Fat: 1 gm., Carbohydrates: 4 gm.

Mix in a food processor and chill:

1 Haas avocado, mashed	**2 Tbsp. cilantro leaves**
2 cups zucchini	**2 Tbsp. lemon juice**
1 cup cherry tomatoes	**1 tsp. Vege-Sal™**
½ cup red onions	

Purifying Vegi-Mole: Substitute dulse powder for Vege-Sal™.

Mushroom Pate

Yield: 6 servings

Per Serving: Calories: 38, Protein: 3 gm., Fat: 0 gm., Carbohydrates: 10 gm.

Saute together until tender:

4 cups sliced mushrooms	**2 Tbsp. liquid aminos**
3 cups diced white onions	**2 tsp. thyme**

Blend in a food processor. Garnish with parsley sprigs.

Salsa Dip

Yield: about 1¼ cups

Per 2 Tablespoons: Calories: 21, Protein: 2 gm., Fat: 1 gm.,
Carbohydrates: 3 gm.

Mix:

1 cup Yogurt Cheese (pg. 180)
6 Tbsp. Pace Salsa™
½ tsp. onion powder

Easy Tortilla Chips

Yield: 8 chips

Per Chip: Calories: 8, Protein: 0 gm., Fat: 0 gm., Carbohydrates: 2 gm.

Cut 1 tortilla into 8 wedge shaped pieces. Cook in a cast iron skillet or griddle until crisp. Add salt or seasonings if desired.

Dolmas

GOURMET

VEGETARIAN

Yield: 16

Per Dolma: Calories: 39, Protein: 1 gm., Fat: 1 gm., Carbohydrates: 7 gm.

Have ready:
   16 grape leaves

Mix together for filling:

**2 cups cooked brown &
   wehani rice mixed
¼ cup currants, soaked in
   2 Tbsp. water**

**2 Tbsp. pine nuts
2 Tbsp. parsley, minced
2 Tbsp. chopped mint leaves
1 tsp. lemon juice**

Rinse grape leaves in water. Put 2 Tbsp. filling in each and roll up tightly. Steam for 10 minutes with a plate on top.

Yogurt Cheese Balls

GOURMET

VEGETARIAN

Yields: 12 balls

Per Cheese Ball: Calories: 50, Protein: 2 gm., Fat: 1 gm., Carbohydrates: 5 gm.

Dry roast together:
   **¾ cups onion flakes
   1½ Tbsp. thyme or basil**

Stir into:
   **1½ cups Yogurt Cheese (pg. 180)
   ¼ cup fresh parsley**

Chill 1-2 hours to develop flavor. Roll into balls, 2 Tbsp. each.

Roll each ball in:
   1 tsp. Toasted Sunnies (pg. 141)

Zesty Mushrooms

Yield: 12

Per Mushroom: Calories: 40, Protein: 2 gm., Fat: 1 gm., Carbohydrates: 7 gm.

Remove stems from 12 jumbo mushrooms. Steam mushrooms for 5 minutes.

Process until well-blended:

2 cups red onions, steamed 10 minutes	**6 Tbsp. toasted bread crumbs**
6 Tbsp. Mustard Sauce (pg. 151)	**3 Tbsp. Parmesan cheese**

Fill each mushroom with:
2 Tbsp. filling

Garnish with:
½ tsp. grated carrot

Serve at room temperature.

Toasted Sunnies

Yield: 2 cups

Per Teaspoon: Calories: 18, Protein: 1 gm., Fat: 0 gm., Carbohydrates: 1 gm.

Preheat oven to 375°.

Stir together:
2 cups sunflower seeds
¼ cup liquid aminos

Bake on a cookie sheet for 45 minutes. Stir every 10-15 minutes.

Dill Dip

Yield: *2½ cups*

Per Tablespoon: Calories: 18, Protein: 2 gm., Fat: 0 gm., Carbohydrates: 3 gm.

Soak in hot water for 6 hours to sprout, then rinse and drain:
2 cups sunflower seeds

Blend until creamy:

**the sprouted sunflower
seeds
½ cup lemon juice
½ cup cucumber
½ cup green pepper**

**¼ cup chopped scallions
⅓ cup liquid aminos
⅓ cup red varietal grape juice
1 Tbsp. dill**

Tofu Chips

Yield: *32 chips*

Per Chip: Calories: 12, Protein: 1 gm., Fat: 1 gm., Carbohydrates: 1 gm.

Preheat oven to 350°.

Cut a into 32 thin slices:
1 lb. tofu

Lay in a baking pan.

Sprinkle with:
**¼ cup liquid aminos
2 Tbsp. nutritional yeast
¼ tsp. onion or garlic powder**

Bake until crisp (about 45 minutes).

SAUCES

Purifying

Health Building

Gourmet Vegetarian

Spaghetti Sauce

Yield: 6½ cups

Per 1 Cup Serving: Calories: 115, Protein: 5 gm., Fat: 0 gm.,
Carbohydrates: 27 gm.

Saute until browned:

1½ cups diced onions	1 tsp. basil
1½ tsp. marjoram	½ tsp. olive oil
1½ tsp. oregano	¼ tsp. rosemary
1½ tsp. garlic	½ bay leaf

Add:
- 3¼ cups tomato puree
- 3¼ cups blended pear tomatoes
- 2 tsp. molasses

Simmer 1-2 hours covered. Can be frozen for use later.

Lo-Cal Savory Sauce

Yield: 1¾ cups

Per Tablespoon: Calories: 18, Protein: 0 gm., Fat: 0 gm., Carbohydrates: 2 gm.

Blend:

1 cup liquid aminos	½ cup nutritional yeast
2 Tbsp. lemon juice	½ tsp. sea dulse powder
1 tsp. basil	½ tsp. Vege-Sal™
½ cup water	

Refrigerate. Keeps well for 1 week. Use on rice, potatoes, vegetables, etc.

Lemon Pepper Sauce

Yield: 1¼ cups

Per Tablespoon: Calories: 15, Protein: 0 gm., Fat: 0 gm., Carbohydrates: 1 gm.

Blend:
   1 cup Tomato Marinade (pg. 152)
   ¼ cup lemon juice
   1 Tbsp. lemon pepper

Orange Glaze

Yield: 1¾ cup

Per Tablespoon: Calories: 13, Protein: 0 gm., Fat: 0 gm., Carbohydrates: 3 gm.

Heat to boiling:
   2 cups orange juice
   1 Tbsp. fructose
   ½ tsp. cinnamon

Mix together and stir into the above:
   2 Tbsp. cornstarch
   ¼ cup water

Cook until thickened (2-3 minutes) stirring constantly. Serve over vegetables.

Pineapple Ginger Glaze

Yield: 1¾ cups

Per Tablespoon: Calories: 13, Protein: 0 gm., Fat: 0 gm., Carbohydrates: 3 gm.

Heat to boiling:
    2 cups pineapple juice   **½ Tbsp. ginger**

Mix together and stir into the above:
    2 Tbsp. cornstarch   **¼ cup water**

Cook until thickened (2-3 minutes) stirring constantly. Serve over vegetables.

Purifying Glaze: Substitute arrowroot for cornstarch.

Sweet & Sour Sauce

Yield: 2½ cups

Per ⅓ Cup Serving: Calories: 62, Protein: 1 gm., Fat: 3 gm.,
                    Carbohydrates: 10 gm.

Mix together in a saucepan:

1 cup water	**4 tsp. liquid aminos**
1 cup unsweetened pineap-	**2 tsp. grated ginger**
ple juice	**¾ tsp. fructose**
½ cup ketchup (pg. 36)	**1½ cloves garlic, minced**
3 Tbsp. rice vinegar	

Bring to a boil.

Mix in a bowl:
    3 Tbsp. cold water   **2 Tbsp. cornstarch**

Whisk slowly into boiling mixture. Turn down to a simmer and cook 3-5 minutes.

Salsa Verde

Yield: 2¾ cups

Per Tablespoon: Calories: 8, Protein: 0 gm., Fat: 0 gm., Carbohydrates: 2 gm.

Cook until soft:
> ½ cup water
> 8 tomatillos
> 2 mild green chilies with seeds removed

Blend.

Add:

> ¾ cup chopped scallions   ½ tsp. garlic powder
> ½ cup cilantro   ½ tsp. Vege-Sal™

Stir all together.

Lemon Pepper Marinade

Yield: 6 cups

Per Tablespoon: Calories: 25, Protein: 0 gm., Fat: 0 gm., Carbohydrates: 1 gm.

Blend:

> 2¼ cups lemon juice   6 Tbsp. fresh parsley
> 1½ cups water or soup   6 Tbsp. olive oil
>   stock   3 Tbsp. onion flakes
> 1 cup apple juice   2 Tbsp. tarragon
> ½ cup tamari   ¾ Tbsp. garlic granules
> ¼ cup white miso   ½ Tbsp. coarse black pepper

Lo-Cal Sunny Sauce

PURIFYING

DIET

Yield: 2½ cups

Per ¼ cup: Calories: 58, Protein: 2 gm., Fat: 1 gm., Carbohydrates: 4 gm.

Soak in hot water for 6 hours to sprout:
1½ cups sunflower seeds

Blend:

the sprouted sunflower seeds	**½ cup celery**
	⅓ cup parsley
½ cup water	**2 tsp. honey**
½ cup soup stock	**1 tsp. dill**
⅓ cup lemon juice	

Keeps well for 2 days.

Cucumber Sauce

HEALTH

BUILDING

Yield: 2 cups

Per ¼ Cup Serving: Calories: 115, Protein: 2 gm., Fat: 1 gm.,
Carbohydrates: 4 gm.

Mix:

2 cups English cucumber strips	**¼ cup lemon juice**
	2 Tbsp. cilantro
1 cup yogurt cheese	
1 cup parsley	

(Salad Dressings) Clockwise from the top: Sour Cream Dill Dressing (pg. 63), Golden Italian Dressing (pg. 170), Cucumber Dressing (pg. 167), Summer Garden Salad Dressing (pg.67), Photographer: Michael Bonnickson, Food Stylist: Louise Hagler

Lemon Caper Sauce

HEALTH

BUILDING

Yield: 3½ cups

Per Tablespoon: Calories: 8, Protein: 0 gm., Fat: 0 gm., Carbohydrates: 1 gm.

Bring to a boil:
1 cup lemon juice
½ cup liquid aminos
2 cups water

Mix together and stir into the above:
¼ cup cornstarch
⅓ cup water

Cook 2 minutes then add:
¼ cup capers
¼ cup caper juice

Serve over vegetables.

Mustard Sauce

HEALTH

BUILDING

Yield: 1 cup

Per Tablespoon: Calories: 17, Protein: 1 gm., Fat: 0 gm., Carbohydrates: 3 gm.

Blend together:
⅓ cup yellow mustard
⅓ cup red miso
⅓ cup sparkling varietal grape juice

Gazpacho (pg. 58) and Tofu Salad in Tomato Flower (pg. 175), Photographer: Alan Parker, Art Director: Mark Allison, Food Stylists: Alan Parker and Jane Buck

Tomato Marinade

Yield: 4 cups

Per Tablespoon: Calories: 18, Protein: 0 gm., Fat: 1 gm., Carbohydrates: 1 gm.

Mix:

1⅓ cup uid aminos	2⅔ Tbsp. safflower oil
⅔ cup water	1 Tbsp. cider vinegar
⅔ cup pineapple juice	1 Tbsp. molasses
⅔ cup ketchup (pg. 36)	3 cloves garlic, minced

Keeps well refrigerated for 2 weeks. If marinade is cooked as a sauce, it becomes *Gourmet Vegetarian*

Miso Mushroom Sauce

Yield: 2½ cups

Per ¼ Cup Serving: Calories: 27, Protein: 1 gm., Fat: 0 gm., Carbohydrates: 6 gm.

Bring to a boil:
2 cups sliced mushrooms
½ cup nonfat milk
½ cup soup stock

Stir in:
¼ cup white miso

Thicken with a mixture of:
¼ cup water
2 Tbsp. cornstarch

Cook 3 more minutes. Remove from heat.

SOUPS

Purifying

Health Building

Gourmet Vegetarian

Soup Stock

Yield: About 10 cups

Put into a 5 qt. pot:
12 cups water

Add:
8 cups assorted vegetables, cut into chunks

Carrots, celery, summer or winter squashes, and onions are a good combination. Cover and bring to a boil. Turn down and simmer 2-4 hours. Strain liquid. Keeps well 3-5 days.

Curried Vegetable Soup

Yield: 4 servings

Per Serving: Calories: 100, Protein: 4 gm., Fat: 0 gm., Carbohydrates: 24 gm.

Combine in a 3 quart pot:

3 cups soup stock	**¾ cup peeled acorn squash cubes**
2 cups cauliflower pieces	**½ cup diced apples**
1 cup apple juice	**¼ cup diced yellow onions**
¾ cup sliced carrots	

Bring to a boil, cover and turn to simmer.

When vegetables are soft, take 2 cups of liquid and blend with:
½ tsp. cumin
¼ tsp. cardamon
¼ tsp. coriander

Add just before serving:
1½ cups tomato wedges

Mushroom Barley Soup

HEALTH

BUILDING

Yield: 5 servings

Per Serving: Calories: 140, Protein: 6 gm., Fat: 0 gm., Carbohydrates: 31 gm.

Combine in a 4 quart pot:

7½ cups soup stock	¼ cup liquid aminos
1¼ cup barley	⅜ tsp. thyme
1 cup sliced yellow squash	⅜ tsp. basil
¾ cup diced white onion	⅜ tsp. tarragon
¾ cup sliced celery	1 small clove garlic, minced

Bring to a boil, cover and turn down to simmer. Cook until barley is tender (about 1½ hours).

Add 5 minutes before serving:
5 cups sliced mushrooms

Green Bean Barley Soup: Use 6 cups green beans in place of mushrooms.

Lo-Cal Smokey Lentil Soup

HEALTH

BUILDING

Yield: 5 servings

Per Serving: Calories: 60, Protein: 6 gm., Fat: 0 gm., Carbohydrates: 7 gm.

Combine in a 4 quart pot:

6 cups soup stock	1 small clove of garlic, minced
2 cup lentils, sprouted	¼ Tbsp. basil
½ cup diced yellow onion	1½ Tbsp. parsley
½ cup diced carrots	1 Tbsp. liquid smoke
½ cup sliced celery	¾ Tbsp. vinegar
¼ cup liquid aminos	

Bring to a boil, cover and turn down to simmer. Cook until lentils are soft (about 1 hour).

Tofu Noodle Soup

GOURMET
VEGETARIAN

Yield: 4 servings

Per Serving: Calories: 132, Protein: 7 gm., Fat: 3 gm., Carbohydrates: 23 gm.

Preheat oven to 350°.

Bake for 20 minutes:
**¾ cup tofu cubes in
3 Tbsp. liquid aminos**

Bring to a boil:
4½ cups of soup stock

Add:
**1¼ cups cooked noodles
tofu cubes**

Mix until dissolved:
**4 Tbsp. yellow miso
2 cups hot soup stock**

Add to remaining ingredients. Serve immediately.

Garnish each with:
1 Tbsp. chopped scallions.

Miso Hiziki Soup

HEALTH
BUILDING

Yield: 6 servings

Per Serving: Calories: 53, Protein: 2 gm., Fat: 0 gm., Carbohydrates: 13 gm.

Soak together for 30 minutes:
**9 cups soup stock
4 Tbsp. hiziki**

Add:
3 cups slant cut carrots

Bring to a boil.

Add 2 cups of this liquid to:
6 Tbsp. of red miso

Blend until dissolved. Add into remaining stock. Serve immediately. Do not boil miso.

Lo-Cal Minestrone

Yield: 8 servings

Per Serving: Calories: 125, Protein: 6 gm., Fat: 1 gm., Carbohydrates: 22 gm.

Bring to a boil:

5 cups soup stock
1 cup bean cooking water
1 cup cooked spaghetti squash
1 cup cooked rainbow spiral noodles

¾ cup garbanzos
¾ cup cooked kidney beans
1½ Tbsp. Spike Seasoning™

Add:

2½ cups diced tomatoes (optional)
2 cups green beans in ½" pieces

Cook 3 more minutes.

Add just before serving:

1 cup fresh parsley
3 Tbsp. red miso

Creamy Carrot Soup

Yield: 6 servings

Per Serving: Calories: 46, Protein: 1 gm., Fat: 0 gm., Carbohydrates: 9 gm.

Boil together until tender:
   6 cups carrot
   6 cups soup stock

Blend small amounts at a time until smooth.

Stir in just before serving:
   ½ tsp. cinnamon

Tomato Bisque

Yield: 6 servings

Per Serving: Calories: 50, Protein: 2 gm., Fat: 0 gm., Carbohydrates: 11 gm.

Bring to a boil:
   4 cups soup stock   **1½ Tbsp. Spike Seasoning**™
   4 cups tomato juice   **2 tsp. Vege-Sal**™
      or 8 ripe cherry tomatoes   **1 lemon, cut in quarters**
   1 Tbsp. dill

Remove lemon.

Mix:
   ⅓ cup cold water
   ⅙ cup cornstarch

Add to soup and stir 3 minutes. Pour into bowls and chill. Serve with a lemon twist.

Variation: Substitute 4 cups ripe cherry tomatoes for 2 cups of juice. After cooking, cool slightly. Then blend (no need to thicken with cornstarch).

Lo-Cal French Onion Soup

GOURMET

VEGETARIAN

Yield: 4 servings

Per Serving: Calories: 100, Protein: 4 gm., Fat: 4 gm., Carbohydrates: 14 gm.

Heat a cast iron skillet or pot until it is very hot.

Add:

3 cups sliced yellow onions	½ Tbsp. thyme
1 ½ Tbsp. butter	½ bay leaf

Stir well until onions are brown.

Add:

3 cups soup stock
½ cup liquid aminos

Heat to serving temperature.

Garlic Soup

HEALTH

BUILDING

Yield: 4 servings

Per Serving: Calories: 60, Protein: 12 gm., Fat: 0 gm., Carbohydrates: 10 gm.

Bring to a boil:

4 cups soup stock	2½ cloves of garlic, minced
1 cup grated potato	1¼ Tbsp. Spike Seasoning™
¼ cup liquid aminos	

Turn to simmer. Cover and cook for 20-30 minutes.

Add at the end:
2 cups Swiss chard, chopped, no stems

Lo-Cal Split Pea Soup

HEALTH BUILDING

Yield: 12 servings

Per Serving: Calories: 125, Protein: 7 gm., Fat: 0 gm., Carbohydrates: 21 gm.

Rinse:
   2 cups green split peas

Add to:

12 cups soup stock	**1½ tsp. vinegar**
1½ cups diced carrots	**2½ tsp. thyme**
1½ cup sliced celery	**1 bay leaf**
¾ cup diced yellow onions	**2 cloves garlic, minced**
¼ cup liquid aminos	

Bring to a boil. Turn to low heat. Cover and simmer 2½ hours. Remove bay leaf before serving.

Creamy Asparagus Soup

HEALTH BUILDING

Yield: 6 servings

Per Serving: Calories: 60, Protein: 5 gm., Fat: 0 gm., Carbohydrates: 15 gm.

Cook together until tender:

6 cups asparagus pieces	**3 cups soup stock**
(set the tips aside)	**1 Tbsp. Spike Seasoning™**
3 cups sliced leeks	**¼ cup liquid aminos**

Pulse in the blender (strain if the asparagus is very fibrous).

Add:
   6 cups asparagus tips

Cook 5 minutes more before serving.

Leek-Corn Chowder

HEALTH
BUILDING

Yield: 8 servings

Per Serving: Calories: 94, Protein: 5 gm., Fat: 0 gm., Carbohydrates: 25 gm.

Cook together until tender:
   8 cups sliced leeks
   6 cups soup stock
   ¼ cup liquid aminos

Then add:
   4 cups corn kernels
   1½ cups celery

Cook 5 more minutes.

Stir in:
   1 tsp. Vege-Sal™

Serve.

Borscht

HEALTH
BUILDING

Yield: 6 servings

Per Serving: Calories: 77, Protein: 3 gm., Fat: 0 gm., Carbohydrates: 18 gm.

Bring to a boil:

5½ cups grated beets	**1 Tbsp. apple cider vinegar**
5½ cups soup stock	**1 Tbsp. dill**
2¾ cups sliced red onion	**1 Tbsp. caraway**
2½ Tbsp. lemon juice	**¾ tsp. Vege-Sal™**

Reduce to a simmer. Cover and cook one hour. Serve hot or chilled.

Cucumber Soup

Yield: 6 servings

Per Serving: Calories: 60, Protein: 3 gm., Fat: 3 gm., Carbohydrates: 6 gm.

Blend together:

2 cups cucumber	**1 Tbsp. dill**
1½ cups lowfat yogurt	**2 Tbsp. lemon juice**
½ cup buttermilk	

Pour into a serving bowl and stir in:
2 cups diced cucumbers

Lo-Cal Gazpacho

Yield: 4 servings

Per Serving: Calories: 61, Protein: 2 gm., Fat: 1 gm., Carbohydrates: 10 gm.

Pulse in a blender:

2⅔ cups fresh tomatoes	**2 tsp. olive oil**
1 cup tomato juice	**1 tsp. lemon juice**
⅔ cup red onion	**½ tsp. celery seed**
4½ Tbsp. parsley	**¼ tsp. Tabasco**
4 tsp. vinegar of your choice	

Chill. Garnish with sliced scallions.

SALAD DRESSINGS

Purifying

Health Building

Gourmet Vegetarian

Lo-Cal Bleu Cheese Dressing

Yield: 1¾ cups

Per Tablespoon: Calories: 17, Protein: 1 gm., Fat: 1 gm., Carbohydrates: 1 gm.

Blend:

1¼ cup buttermilk	1 Tbsp. fresh chives
¾ cup bleu cheese	¼ tsp. garlic powder
1 Tbsp. fresh parsley	⅜ tsp. white pepper

Best if chilled several hours before serving.

Avocado Lime Dressing

Yield: 2¼ cups

Per Tablespoon: Calories: 11, Protein: 0 gm., Fat: 0 gm., Carbohydrates: 1 gm.

Blend:

1 cup buttermilk	3 Tbsp. lime juice
1 avocado	¼ tsp. Vege-Sal™
6 Tbsp. white varietal grape juice	⅛ tsp. nutmeg
	½ tsp. celery seeds

Sesame Dressing

Yield: 2¼ cups

Per Tablespoon: Calories: 29, Protein: 0 gm., Fat: 1 gm., Carbohydrates: 2 gm.

Blend:

1 cup water	2 Tbsp. honey
½ cup peeled apple chunks	1 Tbsp. safflower oil
¼ cup white vinegar	1 Tbsp. sesame oil
¼ cup rice vinegar	½ Tbsp. toasted sesame seeds
3½ Tbsp. tomato paste	

Lo-Cal Italian Dressing

HEALTH
BUILDING

Yield: 1¼ cups

Per Tablespoon: Calories: 17, Protein: 0 gm., Fat: 0 gm., Carbohydrates: 1 gm.

Blend:

¾ cup pureed pear tomatoes	⅜ tsp. basil
2 Tbsp. olive oil	⅜ tsp. marjoram
2 Tbsp. water	⅜ tsp. tarragon
2 Tbsp. rice vinegar	⅛ tsp. Vege-Sal™
2 Tbsp. red wine vinegar	

Lo-Cal Ginger Tamari Dressing

HEALTH
BUILDING

Yield: 2½ cups

Per Tablespoon: Calories: 8, Protein: 0 gm., Fat: 0 gm., Carbohydrates: 2 gm.

Soak for 1 minute:
2 cups water
½ tsp. agar granules

Bring to a boil for 1 minute. Remove from heat.

Blend with:
6 Tbsp. rice vinegar
2 Tbsp. grated ginger

Strain.

Add:
¼ cup honey
2 Tbsp. tamari

Blend again. Refrigerate before serving.

Lemon Tahini Dressing

HEALTH

BUILDING

Yield: 1 cup

Per Tablespoon: Calories: 17, Protein: 1 gm., Fat: 0 gm., Carbohydrates: 1 gm.

Blend:

½ cup celery, sliced   2 Tbsp. green pepper, chopped
¼ cup lemon juice   2 Tbsp. red onion, chopped
¼ cup soup stock   ½ Tbsp. liquid aminos
2 Tbsp. tahini

Savory Dressing

HEALTH

BUILDING

Yield: 1¾ cup

Per Tablespoon: Calories: 7, Protein: 0 gm., Fat: 0 gm., Carbohydrates: 2 gm.

Blend:

⅔ cup liquid aminos   7 Tbsp. lemon juice
⅓ cup nutritional yeast   1 tsp. basil
⅓ cup water

Strawberry Vinegar Dressing

HEALTH

BUILDING

Yield: 3 cups

Per Tablespoon: Calories: 3, Protein: 0 gm., Fat: 0 gm., Carbohydrates: 1 gm.

Blend:

2 cups strawberry preserves (unsweetened)
1½ cups red wine vinegar

Cucumber Dressing

Yield: 2½ cups
See photo, page 149.

Per Tablespoon: Calories: 2, Protein: 0 gm., Fat: 0 gm., Carbohydrates: 0 gm.

Blend until smooth:
¾ cup cucumber, sliced	¾ tsp. dillweed
¼ cup red varietal grape juice	½ tsp. ginger, grated
	¼ tsp. celery seed
3 Tbsp. liquid aminos	1 small clove garlic

Cucumber Vinaigrette Dressing

Yield: 1 cup

Per Tablespoon: Calories: 10, Protein: 0 gm., Fat: 1 gm., Carbohydrates: 1 gm.

Blend:
½ cup Tomato Marinade (pg. 52)	¾ tsp. dillweed
¼ cup cucumber	¼ tsp. celery seeds

Tarragon Dressing

Yield: 2¼ cups

Per 2 Tablespoons: Calories: 16, Protein: 1 gm., Fat: 0 gm., Carbohydrates: 4 gm.

Blend until smooth:
1¾ cup artichoke hearts
1 cup ruby varietal grape juice
½ cup lemon juice
1 Tbsp. tarragon

Lime Dressing

PURIFYING

DIET

Yield: 1½ cups

Per Tablespoon: Calories: 5, Protein: 0 gm., Fat: 0 gm., Carbohydrates: 1 gm.

Blend:

⅜ cup soup stock
½ cup lime juice

½ cup white varietal grape juice
1 Tbsp. basil

Vinaigrette Dressing

HEALTH

BUILDING

Yield: 3 cups

Per Tablespoon: Calories: 4, Protein: 0 gm., Fat: 0 gm., Carbohydrates: 1 gm.

Blend:

2 cups bean sprouts
1½ cups grated carrot
¾ cup rice vinegar
¾ cup soup stock
½ cup apple juice
½ cup celery leaves
2 Tbsp. fresh parsley
1 Tbsp. tamari
1 Tbsp. chopped scallions
   or watercress
1 tsp. miso mustard
1 tsp. basil
½ tsp. fresh rosemary
½ tsp. celery seeds

Fresh Herb Dressing

PURIFYING

DIET

Yield: 1½ cups

Per Tablespoon: Calories: 6, Protein: 0 gm., Fat: 0 gm., Carbohydrates: 1 gm.

Blend together in a blender:

1 cup cucumber
¾ cup celery
½ cup red varietal grape juice
½ cup fresh chives

½ cup fresh parsley
2 Tbsp. lemon juice
¾ tsp. powdered dulse seaweed

Mushroom Vinaigrette

GOURMET

VEGETARIAN

Yield: 2½ cups

Per Tablespoon: Calories: 14, Protein: 0 gm., Fat: 0 gm., Carbohydrates: 1 gm.

Saute together until just soft (about 5 minutes):

3 cups button mushrooms
½ cup ruby varietal grape juice
¼ cup rice vinegar

¼ cup tamari
2 Tbsp. olive oil

Blend together with:

1 cup grated carrot
1 cup grated daikon radish
½ cup lime juice

Sparkling Miso Dressing

GOURMET

VEGETARIAN

Yield: scant one cup

Per Tablespoon: Calories: 10, Protein: 1 gm., Fat: 0 gm., Carbohydrates: 1 gm.

Combine in a food processor:

⅜ **cup sparkling white**
   grape juice
   or sparkling apple juice
¼ **lb. (½ cup) tofu**
1 **Tbsp. brown rice vinegar**
½ **Tbsp. safflower oil**

2¼ **tsp. red miso**
¾ **tsp. toasted sesame oil**
¼ **tsp. ginger powder**
⅛ **tsp. garlic powder**

Golden Italian Dressing

PURIFYING

DIET

Yield: 2½ cups
See photo, page 149.

Per Tablespoon: Calories: 54, Protein: 0 gm., Fat: 6 gm., Carbohydrates: 1 gm.

Blend until smooth:

1 **cup cold pressed oil**
¾ **cup apple juice**
¾ **cup lemon juice**
½ **stalk celery**
1 **medium onion, chopped**
¼ **green pepper**

¾ **Tbsp. marjoram**
2 **tsp. basil**
1¼ **tsp. thyme**
½ **tsp. black pepper**
3 **cloves garlic**

SALADS

Health Building

Gourmet Vegetarian

Potpourri Salad

HEALTH BUILDING

Yield: 6 servings

Per Serving: Calories: 75, Protein: 7 gm., Fat: 0 gm., Carbohydrates: 14 gm.

Steam for 5 minutes:
   3 cups brussel sprouts, cut in half

Combine with:
   3 cups small broccoli flowers
   3 cups raw tender asparagus, cut in 1″ pieces
   ¾ cup Savory Dressing (pg. 166)

Serve on a bed of lettuce. Garnish with a radish rose.

Variations: Substitute equal amount of small cauliflower pieces, steamed 4 minutes, for broccoli. Substitute equal amount of pearl onions, steamed 3 minutes, for brussel sprouts.

Confetti Salad

GOURMET VEGETARIAN

Yield: 6 servings

Per Serving: Calories: 116, Protein: 6 gm., Fat: 1 gm., Carbohydrates: 13 gm.

Marinate 2–4 hours in 6 oz. **Lo-Cal Italian Dressing** (pg. 165):

3 cups small cauliflower pieces, steamed 5 minutes	**¾ cup red onion rings**
	¾ cup red pepper strips
	¾ cup canned baby corn
1½ cups sprouted lentils	

Toss with 6 cups lettuce just before serving.

Missing Bean Salad

HEALTH

BUILDING

Yield: *four 1-cup servings*

Per Serving: *Calories: 107, Protein: 5 gm., Fat: 1 gm., Carbohydrates: 13 gm.*

Mix:

2 cups fresh green beans,
steamed 5 minutes
1 cup cooked kidney beans
½ cup thin sliced red onion
½ cup fresh parsley,
minced

1½ Tbsp. olive oil
1½ Tbsp. rice vinegar
1½ red wine vinegar
¾ Tbsp. Spike Seasoning™

Toss and chill before serving.

Ginger Mint Coleslaw

HEALTH

BUILDING

Yield: *4 servings*

Per Serving: *Calories: 90, Protein: 3 gm., Fat: 4 gm., Carbohydrates: 16 gm.*

Mix:

2 cups shredded red cabbage
2 cups shredded green cabbage
2 cups grated carrots
6 mint leaves

Blend and toss with vegies:

¼ cup lemon juice
¼ cup varietal grape juice
3 Tbsp. Nasoya Mayonnaise™
2 Tbsp. ginger juice

South of the Border Salad

HEALTH
BUILDING

Yield: eight ½-cup servings

Per Serving: Calories: 23, Protein: 1 gm., Fat: 0 gm., Carbohydrates: 5 gm.

Mix:

3 cups diced jicama	½ cup mint leaves
1 cup green pepper sliced thin	¼ cup diced sweet red pepper
½ cup fresh parsley, minced	2 Tbsp. lemon juice

Toss and chill before serving.

Snow Pea Salad

GOURMET

VEGETARIAN

Yield: 8 servings

Per Serving: Calories: 92, Protein: 5 gm., Fat: 2 gm., Carbohydrates: 22 gm.

To make marinade, combine:

1 cup pineapple juice	¼ cup tamari
½ cup rice vinegar	1 Tbsp. toasted sesame oil

Pour over:
   4 cups snow peas
   1½ cup bamboo shoots
   1½ cup sweet red pepper strips

Marinate 2-4 hours.

Just before serving add:
   3 cups mung beans sprouts
   1 Tbsp. black sesame seeds

Tofu Salad in a Tomato Flower

HEALTH

BUILDING

Yield: 6 servings

Per Serving: Calories: 175, Protein: 15 gm., Fat: 8 gm., Carbohydrates: 14 gm.

To make salad, crumble:
4 cups tofu (2 lbs.)

Add:

¾ cup grated carrot	**3 Tbsp. lowfat yogurt**
½ cup chopped green onion	**2 Tbsp. brown rice vinegar**
6 Tbsp. minced pickle	**½ Tbsp. Vege-Sal**™
4 Tbsp. Dijon mustard	**1 tsp. dill**
4 Tbsp. Nasoya	**1 tsp. black pepper**
Mayonnaise™	

Blend well.

Place stem end down:
6 medium sized tomatoes

Slice through to make 6 wedges, leaving them connected at the bottom.

Fill each flower with:
⅔ cup tofu salad

Top each with:
1 green olive

Carrot Crunch Salad

Yield: 6 servings

Per Serving: Calories: 89, Protein: 2 gm., Fat: 1 gm., Carbohydrates: 17 gm.

Mix together:

1½ cup grated carrot	¼ cup lowfat yogurt
1 cup mashed mangos	pinch cumin
¾ cup sprouted wheat berries	pinch cayenne
¼ cup coconut	

Pasta Salad

Yield: 6 servings

Per Serving: Calories: 98, Protein: 3 gm., Fat: 2 gm., Carbohydrates: 14 gm.

Toss:

2 cups cooked multi-colored vegetable rotelli noodles
1⅔ cups sliced celery
2 Tbsp. red wine vinegar
1 Tbsp. Nasoya Mayonnaise™
2 tsp. olive oil
½ tsp. Vege-Sal™
⅛ tsp. black pepper
4 peperincinis
4 green olives

Strawberry Radicchio Salad

HEALTH BUILDING

Yield: 6 servings

Per Serving: Calories: 17, Protein: 1 gm., Fat: 0 gm., Carbohydrates: 4 gm.

Toss:
> **4 cups curly endive**
> **2 cups radicchio**
> **1 cup sliced mushrooms**

With:
> **½ cup Strawberry Vinegar Dressing (pg. 166)**

Wild Rice Salad

HEALTH BUILDING

Yield: 6 servings
See photo page 199.

Per Serving: Calories: 70, Protein: 20 gm., Fat: 0 gm., Carbohydrates: 80 gm.

Toss:
> **2 cups asparagus, ¼″ pieces—steamed 1 minute**
> **2 cups sliced Belgium endive**
> **1 cup cooked wild rice**
> **½ cup sliced scallions**
> **6 oz. Savory Dressing (pg. 166)**

Place in the middle of a platter surrounded by Belgium endive leaves with asparagus spears (steamed 3 minutes) and radish roses, red and white.

ENTREES

Health Building

Gourmet Vegetarian

Low Fat Yogurt

HEALTH

BUILDING

Yield: 3 cups

Per 1 Cup Serving: Calories: 144, Protein: 9 gm., Fat: 3 gm.,
Carbohydrates: 14 gm.

Blend 1 minute:

2 cups lowfat milk
½ cup nonfat milk

¼ cup lowfat yogurt
¼ cup nonfat, non-instant milk
powder

Cook this mixture in a double boiler, whisking until the temperature reaches 115°. Cover and set on a warm counter or in an oven with a pilot light. Check for firmness in 4-6 hours. Refrigerate.

Yogurt Cheese

HEALTH

BUILDING

Yield: about 2 cups

Per Cup: Calories: 192, Protein: 13 gm., Fat: 8 gm., Carbohydrates: 17 gm.

This is a good low calorie substitute for cream cheese.

Line a strainer or collander with a double layer of cheesecloth. Suspend over a bowl to catch the draining liquid.

Pour in:

4 cups lowfat yogurt

Cover and let sit for 24-36 hours until it has a consistency similar to cream cheese. Remove the "cheese" from the cloth and refrigerate. This will keep well for 7-10 days, and has a tangy taste. Blend with chives or herbs to season; also can be combined with fruits and juices.

Four Seasons Quiche

GOURMET

VEGETARIAN

Yield: 6 servings

Per Serving: Calories: 200, Protein: 15 gm., Fat: 8 gm., Carbohydrates: 18 gm.

Preheat oven to 425°.

For crust, mix together:

½ cup whole wheat flour	**1 Tbsp. safflower oil**
4 Tbsp. cold water	**⅛ tsp. salt**

Pat into an 8″ pie pan. Prick with a fork in several places. Pre-bake for 15 minutes. When crust is done, turn oven down to 325°.

For filling, blend in a food processor:
- **1 cup lowfat cottage cheese**
- **½ cup nonfat milk**
- **3 Tbsp. egg replacer**
- **½ cup Yogurt Cheese (pg. 180)**

Stir in:

4 cups seasonal vegetables, prepared according to the list below	**2 Tbsp. onion flakes**
	4 oz. grated lowfat Swiss cheese
2 Tbsp. parsley flakes	

Seasonal Vegetables
1. Asparagus, cut in 1″ pieces and steamed for 5 minutes.
2. Zucchini, raw, grated - blot with paper towel to absorb moisture.
3. Broccoli flowers, steamed 2 minutes.
4. Mushrooms, sliced (start with 4 cups, since they shrink), sauteed in 2 Tbsp. liquid aminos.
5. Artichoke hearts may also be used, add 10 calories per serving.
6. Add 2 Tbsp. hickory bits for another variation, add 10 calories per serving.

Pour into pre-baked pie shell. Bake 45-50 minutes.

Whole Grain Quiche Crust: Mix together 1 cup toasted whole grain bread crumbs, 2 Tbsp. tomato juice and ¼ tsp. garlic. Press into 8″ pie pan.

Cucumber Triangles

Yield: 1 serving

Per Serving: Calories: 149, Protein: 7 gm., Fat: 3 gm., Carbohydrates: 22 gm.

Toast:
   1 slice pumpernickel bread

(Dimpflmeier 100% Rye Plus™ brand rye bread is a good choice if you are looking for an oil and wheat-free rye bread.)

Spread with mixture of:

¼ cup yogurt cheese	**1 Tbsp. fresh basil, chopped**
2 Tbsp. fresh snipped chives	**1 Tbsp. fresh minced parsley**
2 Tbsp. chopped black olives	**1 Tbsp. diced red pimento**

Top with:
   4 cucumber slices
   4 sprigs watercress

Cut into 4 triangles.

Vegetable Puffs

Yield: 8 servings

Per Serving: Calories: 108, Protein: 8 gm., Fat: 2 gm., Carbohydrates: 8 gm.

Have ready:
   8-1 cup ramekins or glass baking dishes
   6 cups pre-steamed vegetables of your choice
   3 Tbsp. toasted bread crumbs

Preheat oven to 350°.

Blend in a food processor:

2 cups lowfat cottage cheese	**2 Tbsp. pimento, diced**
½ cup fresh minced parsley	**1 Tbsp. marjoram**
2 Tbsp. egg replacer	**1 tsp. Vege-Sal™**

Place ¾ cup of pre-steamed vegetables in each baking dish. Pour ⅓ cup of the cottage cheese mixture over each and sprinkle each with 1 tsp. toasted bread crumbs. Bake 20-25 minutes.

Reuben Sandwich

Yield: 1 serving

Per Serving: Calories: 290, Protein: 11 gm., Fat: 5 gm., Carbohydrates: 28 gm.

Preheat oven to 350°.

Cut in half:
1 whole wheat English muffin

On each half spread:
½ oz. lowfat cheese (Swiss)	**1 tsp. Dijon mustard or miso**
¼ cup drained sauerkraut	**mustard**
	1 slice tomato

Bake for 20 minutes. Scooping out part of the muffin will reduce the calories. Rinse the sauerkraut to reduce sodium.

Vegetable Platter

Yield: 1 serving

Per Serving: Calories: 266, Protein: 22 gm., Fat: 3 gm., Carbohydrates: 43 gm.

Blend in the food processor:
½ cups lowfat cottage cheese
½ Tbsp. Spike Seasoning™

Arrange on a platter:
3 lemon wedges	**⅓ cup steamed zucchini**
2 wasa crispbread (rye or	**and/or yellow squash**
savory sesame)	**⅓ cup steamed carrots**
1 artichoke	**and/or beets**
the cottage cheese mix	**¼ cup Savory Dressing (pg. 166)**
⅓ cup steamed broccoli	**¼ cup Mushroom Pate (pg. 139)**
and/or cauliflower	

Great with a cup of soup!

Stuffed Baked Potato

GOURMET
VEGETARIAN

Yield: 8 servings

Per Serving: Calories: 130, Protein: 8 gm., Fat: 1 gm., Carbohydrates: 20 gm.

Preheat oven to 350°.

Bake 6 baking potatoes. Slice in half lengthwise and scoop out potato. Save 8 of the skins.

Combine:

5 cups small broccoli flowers, steamed 1 minute

4½ cups potato

10 Tbsp. Parmesan cheese

1¼ tsp. Vege-Sal™

Measure ½ cup filling into each potato skin. Bake 15-20 minutes.

Top with:

2 Tbsp. fresh snipped chives

Pocket Sandwiches

GOURMET
VEGETARIAN

Yield: 6 servings

Per Serving: Calories: 215, Protein: 10 gm., Fat: 1 gm., Carbohydrates: 26 gm.

Mix together:

1 cup Fantastic Falafel Mix™
¾ cup water

Let stand 15 minutes.

Preheat oven to 375°.

Form into 12 patties, 2 Tbsp. each. Bake 20-25 minutes.

Cut into halves:

3 loaves pocket bread

Warm in the oven.

Put in each warm half:

2 falafel patties
1 cup alfalfa sprouts
5 Tbsp. Cucumber Sauce

Murrieta Chili

HEALTH

BUILDING

Yield: 5 servings

Per Serving: Calories: 235, Protein: 15 gm., Fat: 5 gm., Carbohydrates: 37 gm.

Preheat oven to 350°.

Bake together for 30 minutes:
   ¼ lb. tempeh, crumbled
   1 Tbsp. liquid aminos

Combine in a large saucepan:

3¾ cups cooked pinto
   beans
1 cup liquid from beans
1 cup celery, sliced
1 cup green chilies,
   chopped
1 cup yellow onions,
   chopped
¾ cup tomato chunks

½ cup tomato juice
½ cup tomato paste
½ Tbsp. chili blend
½ Tbsp. garlic powder
¾ tsp. Vege-Sal™

Simmer until celery is tender, add tempeh and serve.

Tofu Chili: Substitute ¼ lb. tofu plus ½ cup corn for tempeh.

Lo-Cal Cottage Roll

GOURMET

VEGETARIAN

Yield: 1 serving

Per Serving: Calories: 231, Protein: 15 gm., Fat: 5 gm., Carbohydrates: 23 gm.

Preheat oven to 350°.

Mix together:
   ⅓ cup lowfat cottage cheese
   ¼ tsp. Spike Seasoning™

¼ tsp. dill
½ oz. Mozzarella cheese

Roll in a chapati and bake 20 minutes.

Tostada

Yield: 6 tostadas

Per Tostada: Calories: 234, Protein: 6 gm., Fat: 1 gm., Carbohydrates: 33 gm.

To make tostada beans, mash:
> **2 cups cooked pinto or kidney beans**
> **1 Tbsp. liquid aminos**
> **½ tsp. cumin**

To make tostada shells, heat a cast iron skillet. Cook one at a time until slightly crisp:
> **6 corn tortillas**

Spread ⅓ cup tostada beans on each tostada shell.

Top with:
> **¾ cup shredded lettuce**
> **⅓ cup Vegimole (pg. 138)**
> **2 Tbsp. onion dip**
> **1 Tbsp. salsa**
> **1 red pepper ring**

Chili Tostadas: Substitute ⅓ cup **Murrieta Chili** (pg. 185) for the tostada beans.

Spinach Lasagne

Yield: 12 servings

Per Serving: Calories: 238, Protein: 18 gm., Fat: 6 gm., Carbohydrates: 20 gm.

Preheat oven to 350°.

Boil until al dente:
> **12 lasagne noodles, 11″ long (sesame wheat noodles)**

Have ready:
> **2 cups Enrico's Spaghetti Sauce™**

Mix together:
> **3 cups lowfat cottage**   **¼ cup Parmesan cheese**
> **cheese**   **1 tsp. basil**

| 2½ cups frozen spinach, thawed and squeezed | ½ tsp. garlic powder |
| ¾ cup chopped yellow onion | 10 oz. grated Mozzarella cheese |

Blend filling ingredients in a food processor.

Layer in a 8½″ x 11″ baking dish in order:
    ½ cup sauce
    4 noodles
    half the spinach mixture
    4 noodles
    ½ cup sauce
    the other half of the spinach mixture
    4 noodles
    1 cup sauce

Top with:
    2 oz. Mozzarella cheese

Bake for 50-60 minutes.

Lo-Cal Tofu Spinach Lasagne: For a dairyless version, substitute 12 oz. soy cheese for the Mozzarella, and 2½ cups tofu cheese for the cottage cheese and Parmesan cheese.

Delicious Kasha Mushroom Casserole

HEALTH

BUILDING

Yield: *4 servings*

Per Serving: *Calories: 255, Protein: 10 gm., Fat: 2 gm., Carbohydrates: 53 gm.*

Preheat oven to 350°.

Layer in a 8½″ x 11″ pan:
    6 cups whole mushrooms, steamed 5 minutes
    2 cups cooked kasha mixed with ¼ cup white miso
    1 ¼ cups acorn squash, cooked and mashed

Bake, covered, about 30 minutes.

Sprinkle with:
    2 Tbsp. roasted pumpkin or sunflower seeds

Cauliflower Bechamel

GOURMET
VEGETARIAN

Yield: 4 servings

Per Serving: Calories: 270, Protein: 17 gm., Fat: 17 gm., Carbohydrates: 23 gm.

Preheat oven to 350°.

To prepare **Bechamel Sauce,** blend in a food processor:

¾ **lb. tofu**	1 **Tbsp. sparkling grape juice**
½ **cup lowfat yogurt**	1 **Tbsp. red miso**
¼ **cup water**	½ **Tbsp. tamari**
2 **Tbsp. tahini**	½ **Tbsp. liquid aminos**
1 **Tbsp. lemon juice**	¾ **tsp. grated ginger**

Layer in a 8½" x 11" pan:

4 **cups cauliflower pieces,**	½ **cup bread crumbs**
steamed 5 minutes	2 **oz. lo-cal cheese**
the sauce	

Bake about 45 minutes.

Millet Patties

GOURMET
VEGETARIAN

Yield: 6 servings

Per Serving: Calories: 192, Protein: 9 gm., Fat: 7 gm., Carbohydrates: 25 gm.

Preheat oven to 350°.

Mix together:

1 **lb. tofu, crumbled**	¼ **cup yellow miso**
2 **cups millet, cooked**	¼ **cup egg replacer**
1 **cup red onion, chopped**	2 **tsp. Vege-Sal**™
1 **cup bell pepper, diced**	1 **tsp. chili blend**
½ **cup ketchup**	

Shape into 12 patties or a loaf and bake 45-50 minutes.

Tropical Fruit Plate

Yield: 1 serving
See photo on cover.

Per Serving: Calories: 300, Protein: 13 gm., Fat: 3 gm., Carbohydrates: 71 gm.

Have ready:

- **7 whole strawberries**
- **2 leaves lettuce**
- **1 kiwi, peeled and sliced**
- **1 slice pineapple (equivalent of 1 cup)**
- **¼ papaya, cut in strips**

- **¼ canteloupe, cut in wedges or balls**
- **⅛ honeydew, cut in wedges or balls**
- **⅓ cup Lo-Cal Angel Sauce (pg. 209)**
- **a mint sprig**

Arrange lettuce leaves on a plate then place pineapple in the center. Arrange remaining fruit around it. Top with **Lo-Cal Angel Sauce** and mint sprig and add lemon and lime wedges. Eat melons first. Wait 10 minutes before eating the rest so melons can digest.

Summer Fruit Plate

Yield: 1 serving

Per Serving: Calories: 312, Protein: 13 gm., Fat: 3 gm., Carbohydrates: 73 gm.

Have ready:

- **2 lettuce leaves**
- **1 small bunch green grapes**
- **1 peach, sliced**
- **10 cherries**

- **½ cup raspberries**
- **½ mango**
- **⅓ cup Lo-Cal Angel Sauce (pg. 209)**

Arrange lettuce leaves on an oval plate. Cut mango lengthwise as close to pit as possible, leaving skin on. Make criss-cross cuts in mango and turn inside out. Place in center of plate and surround with remaining fruit. Top with **Lo-Cal Angel Sauce.**

Artichoke Stuffed with Pine Nuts

HEALTH

BUILDING

Yield: 6 servings

Per Serving: Calories: 180, Protein: 11 gm., Fat: 6 gm., Carbohydrates: 17 gm.

Cut off the top 1½" of six artichokes with a scissors, trim remaining leaves straight across. Steam artichokes until tender, about 30 minutes. While they are steaming, prepare the filling.

Blend well:

1 cup part skimmed ricotta	2 Tbsp. onion flakes
1 cup Yogurt Cheese (pg. 180)	2 Tbsp. red miso

Remove "chokes" and put ⅓ cup filling into each.

Top with:
1 Tbsp. roasted pine nuts

Dairyless Variation: Substitute 6 Tbsp. **Tofu Hummus**
(pg. 136) for ricotta filling.

Eggplant Manicotti

GOURMET

VEGETARIAN

Yield: 6 servings

Per Serving: Calories: 242, Protein: 12 gm., Fat: 7 gm., Carbohydrates: 27 gm.

Preheat oven to 350°.

For filling, mix together:

2 cups pearl onions, steamed 2 minutes	1½ cup part skim ricotta
1½ cups cooked ribbon noodles	2 Tbsp. egg replacer

Slice lengthwise into 12 slices ⅜" thick:
1 large eggplant

Cook 1-2 minutes until soft in:
¾ cup water
4 Tbsp. liquid aminos

Place ¼ cup filling in each slice. Roll and place in a baking dish.

Top with:
1½ cup Enrico's Spaghetti Sauce™

Bake covered 35-40 minutes. Serve garnished with fresh parsley.

Sandwich Spreads &
Baked Potato Toppings

Yield: ½ cup per topping

Per Tablespoon: Calories: 17, Protein: 2 gm., Fat: 1 gm., Carbohydrates: 0 gm.

Blend in the food processor:
½ cup part skim ricotta
1½ tsp. lemon pepper

Per Tablespoon: Calories: 15, Protein: 2 gm., Fat: 1 gm., Carbohydrates: 1 gm.

Blend in the food processor:
¼ cup Yogurt Cheese (pg. 180)
¼ cup part skim ricotta
1 tsp. dill weed

Per Tablespoon: Calories: 18, Protein: 1 gm., Fat: 1 gm., Carbohydrates: 1 gm.

Blend in the food processor:
½ cup Yogurt Cheese (pg. 180)
3 Tbsp. chopped green olives
2 tsp. pimento

Per Tablespoon: Calories: 20, Protein: 2 gm., Fat: 0 gm., Carbohydrates: 0 gm.

Blend in the food processor:
½ cup lowfat cottage cheese
½ Tbsp. Spike Seasoning™

Stuffed Mushrooms

GOURMET

VEGETARIAN

Yield: 6 servings

Per Serving: Calories: 125, Protein: 8 gm., Fat: 1 gm., Carbohydrates: 21 gm.

Preheat oven to 350°.

Remove stems and use a spoon to make a cavity for stuffing in:
3 lbs. jumbo mushrooms

Saute together:
2 cups chopped mushroom stems
½ cup chopped yellow onions
4 Tbsp. liquid aminos

Drain off excess liquids.

Mix in:

1 cup cooked wild rice   **¼ cup fresh chives, snipped into**
½ cup Yogurt Cheese   **small pieces with a scissors**
(pg. 180)

Saute mushroom caps in liquid left from onion and mushroom saute. Add more water if needed. Stuff mushrooms. Bake for 20 minutes.

Cabbage Rolls

GOURMET

VEGETARIAN

Yield: 5 servings

Per Serving: Calories: 207, Protein: 5 gm., Fat: 7 gm., Carbohydrates: 28 gm.

Preheat oven to 350°.

Filling:

1½ cups long grain brown   **¾ cup onion, diced**
rice, cooked   **½ cup tofu, crumbled**
1½ cups cabbage, shredded   **1 Tbsp. toasted sesame oil**
1 cup carrots, grated   **1 Tbsp. liquid aminos**

Saute the onions in the oil until just transparent. Add tofu, cook until slightly browned, then add all other ingredients. Cook until cabbage just begins to wilt.

Steam until soft:
   5 cabbage leaves

Place onto each cabbage leaf:
   ¾ cup filling

Roll up, tucking the sides in as you roll. Place into pan with a lid. Bake about 30 minutes.

Add while baking to each roll:
   ⅓ cup Sweet & Sour Sauce (pg. 146)

Garnish with a total of:
   ¼ cup green onion slices   1 Tbsp. black sesame seeds

Broccoli Chapati Pizza

GOURMET

VEGETARIAN

Yield: 4 servings

Per Serving: Calories: 231, Protein: 3 gm., Fat: 1 gm., Carbohydrates: 7 gm.

Preheat oven to 350°.

Have ready:
   4 whole wheat chapatis

Layer on each chapati:
   ¼ cup grated zucchini   1½ Tbsp. sliced black olives
   2 Tbsp. Spaghetti Sauce   ¾ oz. Mozzarella cheese
   **   (pg. 144)   or lo-cal garlic Jack cheese**

Bake about 15 minutes.

Add to each chapati:
   ⅓ cup broccoli flowers

Variation: Use Oasis Pizza Crust™ with ⅓ of the bread scooped out.

Ratatouille

GOURMET

VEGETARIAN

Yield: 4 servings

Per Serving: Calories: 240, Protein: 8 gm., Fat: 1 gm., Carbohydrates: 43 gm.

Heat a cast iron skillet or pot till hot.

Add:

4 cups eggplant, cubed	**1½ tsp. thyme**
1 cup red onion wedges	**½ tsp. garlic**
4 tsp. olive oil	**2 bay leaves**

Cook, stirring continually, about 5 minutes until almost tender.

Then add:
   4 cups green beans, cut in 1″ pieces
   2 cups red pepper strips

Cook until tender.

Add at the end:
   2 cups tomato wedges
   1 cup fresh parsley

Accompany each serving with:
   ½ cup cooked brown rice or ½ cup cooked ribbon noodles

Stir Fry

GOURMET

VEGETARIAN

Yield: 6 servings

Per Serving: Calories: 266, Protein: 18 gm., Fat: 3 gm., Carbohydrates: 47 gm.

Preheat oven to 350°.

Cut into 18 strips:
   ¾ lb. tofu

Lay the strips in a baking dish with:
   2 Tbsp. liquid aminos
   2 Tbsp. water

Bake for 20 minutes.

Heat together in a skillet or wok:
3 cups slant cut carrots
1 cup water
½ cup liquid aminos

Cook for 5 minutes, then add:
12 cups fresh mung sprouts
3 cups cooked noodles (soba recommended)
1½ cups water chestnuts

Cook 5 more minutes, then add:
8 cups fresh spinach or chard
3 cups whole snow peas

Cook 2 more minutes, add tofu strips and serve.

Spaghetti Squash with Wild Rice

HEALTH

BUILDING

Yield: 6 servings

Per Serving: Calories: 256, Protein: 9 gm., Fat: 1 gm., Carbohydrates: 44 gm.

Cut into large chunks:
3 lbs. spaghetti squash

Steam 20 minutes or until tender. Scoop squash out of skin.

While squash is steaming, mix together:
3 cups cooked brown rice   **6 Tbsp. sunflower seeds, soaked 6**
1½ cup cooked wild rice   **hours in hot water, then drained**
                                                        4 Tbsp. Savory Sauce (pg. 144)

Make a nest of ⅔ cup spaghetti squash in 6 bowls (1½ cup size). Put ¾ cup filling in each. Sprinkle with fresh parsley.

Nori Rolls

HEALTH

BUILDING

Yield: 4 rolls
See photo page 200.

Per Roll: Calories: 125, Protein: 3 gm., Fat: 2 gm., Carbohydrates: 24 gm.

Mix together:

2 cups cooked brown rice	1 Tbsp. tamari
½ cup mung bean sprouts	½ Tbsp. Nasoya Mayonnaise™
½ cup grated carrot	2 tsp. lemon juice
½ cup cucumber, finely diced	3 freshly chopped umeboshi plums
¼ cup daikon radish	1 tsp. dill weed
2 Tbsp. fresh parsley	

Let the mixture sit one or more hours to absorb the flavors.

Set out:
   4 sheets toasted nori

Place ¾ cup filling on each sheet of toasted nori. Roll tightly and cut into 5 slices.

Rainy Day Stew

HEALTH

BUILDING

Yield: 6 servings

Per Serving: Calories: 242, Protein: 8 gm., Fat: 0 gm., Carbohydrates: 49 gm.

Preheat oven to 400°.

For gravy, blend together:

2 cups red varietal grape juice	1 Tbsp. thyme
2 cups soup stock	1 Tbsp. garlic
¼ cup red miso	2 tsp. sage
	2 tsp. rosemary

Arrange in a covered casserole:
   3 cups potatoes - chunks about ¾" square
   3 cups carrots - chunks about 1" long
   3 cups red onion - half wedges about ½"
   3 cups beets - wedges about ¾"
   2 cups turnips - chunks about ¾" squares

Pour gravy over vegetables and stir. Bake covered for 2 hours. Check and stir twice during this time.

Just before serving add:
1½ cups thawed frozen green peas

Stuffed Squash with Pearls

GOURMET

VEGETARIAN

Yield: 6 servings

Per Serving: Calories: 175, Protein: 5 gm., Fat: 3 gm., Carbohydrates: 30 gm.

Saute until brown:
3 cups sliced yellow onions	**1 Tbsp. thyme**
2 Tbsp. butter	**1 bay leaf**

Add:
3 cups sliced mushrooms

Cook 15 minutes, then blend.

Stir in:
2 cups pearl onions, steamed 2 minutes
2 Tbsp. pumpkin seeds

Spoon into small acorn squash halves, steamed 15 minutes.

Top each with:
½ Tbsp. diced pimentos

Lemon Pepper Kabobs

Yield: 4 servings (8 kabobs)

Per Serving: Calories: 145, Protein: 10 gm., Fat: 3 gm., Carbohydrates: 22 gm.

Preheat oven to 350°.

Marinate in **Lemon Pepper Marinade** (pg. 145) 4-6 hours:

**4 oz. tempeh, cut into 16
squares**
**16 whole button mush-
rooms**
**4 small zucchini cut into 6
rounds each**

**2 small yams cut into 16 wedges -
pre-steam 8 minutes**
1 pearl onion

Drain marinade.

Arrange on a skewer:

3 zucchini pieces
2 tempeh cubes
2 mushrooms

2 onion wedges
2 yam cubes

Bake for 30 minutes. Baste with marinade during baking time.

Lemon Pepper Kabobs (pg. 198) with Wild Rice Salad (pg. 177) and Orange Sorbet (pg. 211), Photographer: Steven Simpson, Food Stylists: Jane Buck and Barbara Maynord

Vegetable Crepes

GOURMET

VEGETARIAN

Yield: 6 servings

Per Serving: Calories: 310, Protein: 17 gm., Fat: 5 gm., Carbohydrates: 46 gm.

Have ready:
   Miso Mushroom Sauce (pg. 152)

For filling, mix together:

3 cups small broccoli flowers, steamed 3 minutes

2 cups snowpeas, cut in thirds, steamed 30 seconds

1¼ cups cooked spinach, drained

1 cup partially skimmed ricotta cheese

½ Tbsp. fresh chopped rosemary

½ tsp. Vege-Sal™

Preheat oven to 350°.

Have ready:
   6 whole wheat chapatis or flour tortillas

Dip each chapati or tortilla in the mushroom sauce. Put 1 cup filling in and roll it up. Arrange in a baking dish and bake 20 minutes. Serve each with ¼ cup sauce.

Nori Rolls (pg. 196), Photographer: Michael Bonnickson, Food Stylist: Louise Hagler

Spinach Touffle

GOURMET

VEGETARIAN

Yield: 6 servings

Per Serving: Calories: 203, Protein: 13 gm., Fat: 11 gm., Carbohydrates: 11 gm.

Preheat oven to 350°.

Thaw and squeeze:
   1¼ cups frozen spinach

Saute:
   1 cup chopped yellow onions
   2 Tbsp. liquid aminos

Blend in food processor:

2 cups tofu (1 lb.)	¾ tsp. marjoram
⅔ cup Yogurt Cheese	¾ tsp. basil
(pg. 180)	½ tsp. Vege-Sal™
½ cup nonfat milk	⅜ tsp. garlic powder
2 Tbsp. oil (almond or	¼ tsp. thyme
safflower)	¼ tsp. nutmeg
1½ Tbsp. liquid aminos	
1 Tbsp. egg replacer	

Stir in spinach and onions. Pour into 9″ pie pan. Bake for 1 hour.

After removing from oven, top with:
   3 oz. grated Mozzarella cheese

Chinese Vegetables

HEALTH

BUILDING

Yield: 6 servings

Per Serving: Calories: 189, Protein: 10 gm., Fat: 0 gm., Carbohydrates: 36 gm.

For sauce, bring to a boil:

3½ cups soup stock	4 Tbsp. grated ginger root
½ cup liquid aminos	1 Tbsp. fructose
¼ cup tamari	

Stir in:
   ½ cup water mixed with
   ⅓ cup cornstarch

Cook 3-5 minutes until thickened.

Pour the sauce over the following vegetables which have been lightly steamed or cooked in a wok:

4 cups slant cut carrots - steamed 5 minutes
4 cups slant cut celery - steamed 3 minutes
4 cups red pepper squares - steamed 2 minutes
4 cups broccoli flowers - steamed 2 minutes
2 cups spaghetti squash - steamed 20 minutes and scooped out of skin
2 cups bamboo shoots
2 cups shitake mushrooms

This can be served over any grain or pasta.

Lo-Cal Tofu Yung

HEALTH

BUILDING

Yield: 5 servings

Per Serving: Calories: 134, Protein: 12 gm., Fat: 5 gm., Carbohydrates: 14 gm.

Preheat oven to 350°.

Blend until creamy in a food processor:
1 lb. tofu

Add this to:

1 cup mung bean sprouts	**¼ cup egg replacer**
½ lb. crumbled tofu	**2 Tbsp. tamari**
½ cup sliced celery	**1 Tbsp. ginger**
½ cup grated carrots	**2 tsp. garlic powder**
½ cup chopped scallions	

Shape into 10 mounds and bake 25-30 minutes. Serve with soba noodles and steamed vegetables.

Adventurer's Kabobs

GOURMET

VEGETARIAN

Yield: 1 serving
See photo on cover.

Per Serving: Calories: 200, Protein: 14 gm., Fat: 6 gm., Carbohydrates: 34 gm.

Have ready:
   Tomato Marinade (pg. 152)

Pour over and marinate for 6-8 hours:
   4 tofu cubes (¼ lb.)
   4 red potato cubes 1¼",
   steam 15 minutes
   4 green pepper squares,
   1¼"

   4 red pepper squares, 1¼"
   4 red onion wedges
   2 cherry tomatoes

Drain. Save marinade. Arrange vegetables on two bamboo skewers.
Barbeque, grill or bake kabobs in a hot oven. Baste with marinade
while cooking.

Tofu Patties

HEALTH

BUILDING

Yield: 8 patties

Per Pattie: Calories: 175, Protein: 11 gm., Fat: 5 gm., Carbohydrates: 10 gm.

Preheat oven to 350°.

Mix together:
   4½ cups crumbled tofu
   (2¼ lbs.)
   ¾ cup chopped scallions
   ¼ cup red miso
   6 Tbsp. onion flakes

   2 Tbsp. egg replacer
   1 Tbsp. thyme
   1 tsp. Vege-Sal™

Form into 8 patties (⅔ cup each) and bake 25-30 minutes.

Tofu Burgers: Make patties ⅓ cup size; serve with small
   dinner rolls as a bun, and add "the works": 1 lettuce leaf, 2 slices
   dill pickle, 1 Tbsp. Nasoya Mayonnaise™, 1 Tbsp. Dijon mustard, 1
   red onion slice and 1 tomato slice.

Spaghetti Balls

GOURMET

VEGETARIAN

Yield: 5 servings

Per Serving: Calories: 281, Protein: 16 gm., Fat: 5 gm., Carbohydrates: 43 gm.

Preheat oven to 350°.

Bake together for 20 minutes:
   1 lb. tofu crumbled
   2 Tbsp. liquid aminos

Then cool.

Mix baked tofu with:

1½ cups steamed eggplant, peeled, mashed & cooled	**½ tsp. celery seed**
	½ tsp. basil
⅓ cup bread crumbs	**½ tsp. marjoram**
⅛ cup parsley	**½ tsp. garlic**
6 Tbsp. diced onion	**½ tsp. Vege-Sal™**
½ Tbsp. egg replacer	

Form into balls. Bake for 45-50 minutes.

Include with a serving of 5 balls:

⅓ cup Spaghetti Sauce (pg. 144) or Enrico's Spaghetti Sauce™	**⅔ cup cooked pasta**
	1 Tbsp. Parmesan cheese

Lo-Cal Enchiladas

GOURMET

VEGETARIAN

Yield: 6 serving

Per Serving: Calories: 278, Protein: 13 gm., Fat: 6 gm., Carbohydrates: 34 gm.

For filling, mix together in a food processor until smooth:
2 cups tofu (1 lb.) crumbled
1 cup Salsa Verde (pg. 147)
¾ cup chopped black olives

For sauce, bring to a boil:

2 cups water	**½ Tbsp. vinegar**
1 Tbsp. chili blend	**1 tsp. cumin**
1 Tbsp. fructose	**¾ tsp. garlic powder**
1 Tbsp. onion powder	**¼ tsp. Vege-Sal™**

Thicken with a mixture of:
¼ cup cold water
2 Tbsp. cornstarch

Cook 3 minutes.

Preheat oven to 350°.

Steam for 1 minute:
8 corn tortillas

Put ¼ cup filling in each roll, arrange in a pan and cover with 1½ cups sauce.

Blend:
1 cup black beans
1 cup enchilada sauce
2 oz. grated lo-cal orange Cheddar cheese

Pour over enchiladas and bake 35-40 minutes.

DESSERTS

Purifying

Health Building

Gourmet Vegetarian

Pineapple Coconut Jell

Yield: 9 servings

Per Serving: Calories: 110, Protein: 1 gm., Fat: 0 gm., Carbohydrates: 28 gm.

Soak together for 2 minutes:
¾ cup water
¾ cup pineapple coconut juice
3 Tbsp. agar granules or ½ cup agar flakes

Cook, stirring constantly for 2-3 minutes.

Remove and add:
4½ cups pineapple coconut juice
2 Tbsp. lemon juice

Pour into a 6 cup mold and refrigerate until firm. Serve with fruit and **Lo-Cal Angel Sauce** (pg. 209).

Lemon-Lime Jell

Yield: 6 servings

Per Serving: Calories: 83, Protein: 0 gm., Fat: 0 gm., Carbohydrates: 22 gm.

Soak together for 2 minutes:
¾ cup water   **3 Tbsp. agar granules or**
¾ cup lemon juice   **½ cup agar flakes**

Stir in:
½ cup fructose

Cook, stirring constantly for 2-3 minutes.

Remove and add:
3¾ cups water   **¾ cup lime juice**

Pour into a 6 cup mold and refrigerate until firm. Serve with fruit and **Lo-Cal Angel Sauce** (pg. 209).

Agar Parfaits

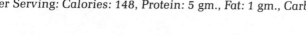

Yield: 1 serving

Per Serving: Calories: 148, Protein: 5 gm., Fat: 1 gm., Carbohydrates: 33 gm.

Layer:
   ½ cup Pineapple-Coconut Jell (pg. 208)
   ½ kiwi, sliced
   3 Tbsp. Lo-Cal Angel Sauce (pg. 209)

Yield: 1 serving

Per Serving: Calories: 152, Protein: 6 gm., Fat: 0 gm., Carbohydrates: 29 gm.

Layer:
   ½ cup Lemon-Lime Jell (pg. 208)
   ½ pear, sliced
   4 Tbsp. Lo-Cal Angel Sauce (pg. 209)

Lo-Cal Angel Sauce

Yield: 5 cups

Per ⅓ Cup Serving: Calories: 80, Protein: 9 gm., Fat: 2 gm.,
                Carbohydrates: 5 gm.

Blend in a food processor until creamy:
   5 cups lowfat cottage cheese
   ¼ cup fructose
   1½ tsp. vanilla

Whipped Topping

HEALTH
BUILDING

Yield: 16 heaping Tbsp.

Per Tbsp.: Calories: 9, Protein: 1 gm., Fat: 0 gm., Carbohydrates: 2 gm.

Place in a small bowl in the freezer for 1-2 hours:
beaters for an electric mixer
½ cup evaporated skim milk

Remove and add:
1 Tbsp. fructose
¼ tsp. vanilla

Whip until fluffy. Serve immediately.

Quick Fruit Whip

HEALTH
BUILDING

Yield: 6 servings

Per Serving: Calories: 36, Protein: 1 gm., Fat: 0 gm., Carbohydrates: 9 gm.

Puree in a food processor:
2 cups kiwi
1 cup mango

Spoon into serving dishes and top with:
1 Tbsp. Lo-Cal Angel Sauce (pg. 209)

Chill before serving.

Orange Sorbet

HEALTH

BUILDING

Yield: 6 servings
See photo, page 199.

Per Serving: Calories: 63, Protein: 1 gm., Fat: 0 gm., Carbohydrates: 12 gm.

Mix:

2 cups fresh orange juice	1 Tbsp. fresh lemon juice
⅔ cups water	1 Tbsp. fructose
⅓ cup fresh carrot juice	1 Tbsp. grated orange rind

Freeze until solid in ice cube trays. Remove from freezer 1 hour before needed. Whip in a food processor. Spoon into serving dishes. Refreeze 30-45 minutes.

Pineapple Mint Sorbet

HEALTH

BUILDING

Yield: 9 servings

Per Serving: Calories: 51, Protein: 0 gm., Fat: 0 gm., Carbohydrates: 13 gm.

Blend together in a blender:
3 cups pineapple juice
1½ cups water
2 Tbsp. mint leaves
1½ Tbsp. lemon juice
¾ Tbsp. fructose

Freeze until solid in ice cube trays. Remove from freezer 1 hour before needed. Whip in food processor then spoon into serving dishes. Refreeze 30-35 minutes.

Coffee Gelato

HEALTH

BUILDING

Yield: 6 servings

Per Serving: Calories: 26, Protein: 1 gm., Fat: 0 gm., Carbohydrates: 5 gm.

Blend:
   1½ cups brewed decaf coffee
   ¾ cup nonfat milk
   2 Tbsp. fructose

Freeze until solid in ice cube trays. Remove from freezer 1 hour before needed. Whip in a food processor. Spoon into serving dishes. Refreeze 30-45 minutes.

Lo-Cal Cheesecake

GOURMET

VEGETARIAN

Yield: 8 servings

Per Serving: Calories: 160, Protein: 9 gm., Fat: 5 gm., Carbohydrates: 21 gm.

Preheat oven to 350°.

Pat into the bottom of a 9″ pie pan:
   ⅓ cup honey graham cracker crumbs

Blend together:
   2 cups part skim ricotta
   1¼ cups nonfat milk
   6 Tbsp. fructose
   3 Tbsp. egg replacer
   1 tsp. vanilla
   ½ tsp. lemon juice

Pour into pie pan. Bake for 30 minutes. Top with fresh fruit, in season.

Strawberry Yogurt Cheese

GOURMET

VEGETARIAN

Yield: 4 cups

Per ¼ Cup Serving: Calories: 38, Protein: 1 gm., Fat: 1 gm., Carbohydrates: 6 gm.

Stir together:
4 cups sliced strawberries
2 Tbsp. fructose

Add to:
1½ cups yogurt cheese

Process until smooth.

Pumpkin Custard

GOURMET

VEGETARIAN

Yield: 6 servings

Per Serving: Calories: 62, Protein: 2 gm., Fat: 0 gm., Carbohydrates: 13 gm.

Preheat oven to 350°.

Blend in a food processor:
1 cup pumpkin puree
1 cup nonfat milk
3 Tbsp. fructose
2 Tbsp. egg replacer
1 tsp. maple flavor
½ tsp. cinnamon
⅛ tsp. cloves

Pour into individual custard cups. Place these into a pan of water. Bake for 1 hour.

Butterscotch Brownies

Yield: 18 brownies

Per Brownie: Calories: 120, Protein: 2 gm., Fat: 3 gm., Carbohydrates: 19 gm.

Preheat oven to 350°.

Mix together:

1 cup fructose	**2 Tbsp. molasses**
½ cup water	**1 Tbsp. maple flavor**
5 Tbsp. melted butter or ghee (pg. 32)	**1 tsp. vanilla**

Stir this into:

1½ cups flour	**2 tsp. baking powder**
¼ cup chopped nuts	**¼ tsp. salt**

Bake in a 10½″ x 5½″ pan lined with waxed paper for 30 minutes.

Carob Brownies

Yield: 18 brownies

Per Brownie: Calories: 130, Protein: 2 gm., Fat: 3 gm., Carbohydrates: 19 gm.

Preheat oven to 350°.

Mix together:

1 cup Tbsp. fructose	**4½ Tbsp. ghee (pg. 32) or melted butter**
⅔ cup water	
¼ cup carob powder	**1 Tbsp. vanilla**

Stir this into:

1½ cups flour	**2 tsp. baking powder**
¼ cup chopped nuts	**¼ tsp. sea salt**

Bake in a 10½″ x 5½″ pan lined with waxed paper for 30 minutes.

Peach Pie

GOURMET

VEGETARIAN

Yield: 8 servings

Per Serving: Calories: 111, Protein: 2 gm., Fat: 3 gm., Carbohydrates: 23 gm.

Preheat oven to 350°.

To prepare crust, lightly toss together and press into bottom of pie pan:

1½ cups bran
1 Tbsp. fructose
1½ Tbsp. safflower oil

Pre-bake 10 minutes.

To prepare filling, bring to a boil:

1½ cups apple juice
2 Tbsp. lemon juice

To prepare sauce mix together and add:

2 Tbsp. water
1½ Tbsp. cornstarch

Stir until thickened (2-3 minutes).

Remove from heat and add:

1 tsp. vanilla

Arrange on top of crust:

5 cups sliced peaches

Pour sauce over them. Chill 1-2 hours before serving.

Lemon Spice Cookies

Yield: 3 dozen

Per Cookie: Calories: 50, Protein: 1 gm., Fat: 2 gm., Carbohydrates: 6 gm.

Preheat oven to 350°.

Cream in a food processor:

1 cup whole wheat pastry flour	1 tsp. grated lemon rind
½ cup unbleached white flour	¼ tsp. cinnamon
¼ cup brown rice syrup	¼ tsp. nutmeg
6 Tbsp. butter	¼ tsp. cloves
3 Tbsp. fructose	¼ tsp. ginger
1 Tbsp. lemon juice	

Remove and stir in:
   1 cup unsweetened bran flake cereal

Use 2 tsp. dough per cookie. Press with a fork and bake 10-12 minutes.

Blueberry Muffins

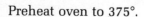

Yield: One dozen

Per Muffin: Calories: 123, Protein: 4 gm., Fat: 1 gm., Carbohydrates: 23 gm.

Preheat oven to 375°.

Combine until crumbly:

1½ cups whole wheat pastry flour	2 Tbsp. butter
½ cup unbleached flour	1 Tbsp. baking powder
¼ cup fructose	½ tsp. sea salt

Add and stir until just moist:
   2 cups fresh blueberries
   1¼ cups buttermilk

Pour into muffin tins lined with cupcake papers. Bake 30-35 minutes.

Carrot Cake

Yield: 15 servings

Per Serving: Calories: 180, Protein: 8 gm., Fat: 4 gm., Carbohydrates: 35 gm.

Preheat oven to 350°.

Mix together in a bowl:

**3 cups whole wheat pastry
flour
2¼ cups wheat bran
1½ tsp. baking soda**

**1 tsp. sea salt
1 tsp. egg replacer**

Add and mix until moistened:

**2 cups grated carrot
2 cups crushed drained
pineapple, unsweetened**

**1⅓ cups buttermilk
⅔ cup honey**

Pour into a pan 8½" x 11" lined with waxed paper. Bake about 1 hour.

Carrot Muffins: Make into 2 dozen muffins (113 calories each). Baking time is 40-45 minutes.

Fudge Date Balls

Yield: 10 balls

Per Ball: Calories: 46, Protein: 1 gm., Fat: 0 gm., Carbohydrates: 13 gm.

Blend in a food processor:

**10 pitted medjool dates
¼ cup toasted carob powder
¼ cup nonfat instant milk powder
3 Tbsp. rice syrup
1½ tsp. vanilla**

Add water if needed. Roll into balls (moisten hands with water to prevent sticking). Refrigerate until serving time. Press 1 slivered almond onto each ball.

Snowballs

HEALTH
BUILDING

Yield: 25 balls

Per Ball: Calories: 37, Protein: 1 gm., Fat: 2 gm., Carbohydrates: 3 gm.

Mix:
2 cups unsweetened coconut
¾ cup instant nonfat dry milk
⅓ cup nonfat milk
¼ cup brown rice syrup
1 tsp. egg replacer

Roll into 25 balls. Store in refrigerator or freezer.

Baked Apple

PURIFYING
DIET

Yield: 1 serving

Per Serving: Calories: 105, Protein: 0 gm., Fat: 0 gm., Carbohydrates: 27 gm.

Preheat oven to 350°.

Core:
1 medium green apple

Soak for 10 minutes in:
½ cup water
½ cup pineapple juice

Put in a baking dish with the juice.

Put in the center:
1 large, fresh pitted date

Sprinkle with:
⅛ tsp. cinnamon

Bake for 1 hour.

APPENDIX

What is 100 Calories?

Computerized Nutritional Analyses

Calorie Chart

What is 100 Calories?

A list to give you a perspective of calorie contents in common ingredients.

2½ tsp. oil
1 Tbsp. butter
1 Tbsp. nut butter
1 oz. cream cheese
4½ dates
2 Tbsp. sunflower seeds
1 oz. Cheddar or Monterey Jack cheese
1¼ oz. lowfat cheese
½ cup lowfat yogurt cheese
½ cup cooked pasta
½ cup lowfat cottage cheese
½ cup cooked rice
½ cup cooked lentils
⅔ cup lowfat yogurt
⅔ cup tofu (⅓ lb.)
¾ cup cooked cream of wheat
1 medium potato (approx. 1 cup)
1 cup cooked oats
9 oz. nonfat milk or buttermilk
1 pear
2½ kiwis or medium peaches
3 cups cooked asparagus
2 artichokes
2½ cups cooked broccoli
6 cups cucumbers
8 cups alfalfa sprouts

Computerized Nutritional Analyses

Nutritional analyses are given for each recipe. Included in each are all ingredients listed by amount, plus typical quantities of basic ingredients not specified by amount, such as oil used in deep-frying. Ingredients not included in the analyses are those such as garnishes, serving suggestions, and variations, which are treated as options. If the recipe serves 4 to 6, the analysis is averaged out to 5 servings. If a certain amount of one or more foods is called for, such as 2 cups brown rice or white rice, the first is included in the reading. Some recipes have their analyses given per unit or by volume, as appropriate.

Calorie Chart

Fruit	Calories	Fruit	Calories
Apple, 1 medium	80	Kiwi, 1	40
Apples, 1 average		Mango, 1 average	30
2½" diameter	80	Nectarine, 1 average	30
dried - 1 cup	101	Orange, 1 average	75
Applejuice, unsweetened	120	juice, 8 oz fresh	120
Applesauce, ½ cup	49	Papaya, ½ cup cubed	36
Apricots, 3 average	55	or ½ cup	60
dried, ½ cup (20 halves)	195	Peaches, 1 average	35
Banana, 1 average	87	dried, ½ cup	210
½ cup slices	64	Pears, 1 average	100
Berries, Black, ½ cup	42	Persimmon, 1 average	81
Blue, ½ cup	43	Pineapple, ½ cup diced	36
Boysen, ½ cup	32	½ cup crushed, canned	70
Rasp, ½ cup	35	juice, unsweetened 8 oz	137
Straw, ½ cup	36	Plums, 1 average	30
or 1 cup	58	Pomegranate, ½ lb.	80
Canteloupe, ½ melon,		Prunes, 1 large dried	19
5" diameter	58	Raisins, 1 oz	80
½ cup diced	36	1 cup	480
Cherries, ½ cup	41	Watermelon, 1 4" x 8" wedge	111
½ lb.	143		
Coconut,		**Sprouts & Vegetables**	**Calories**
½ cup unsweetened	340		
or ½ cup shredded	170	Alfalfa sprouts, 1 oz = 1 cup	12
Cranberries, ½ lb.	100	Artichoke, 1 average	53
Dates, 1 dry	22	whole, cooked	45
½ cup diced	244	Asparagus, ½ cup cooked	18
Figs, 1 small	30	cooked, 6 spears	19
1 large	57	Avocado, ½ average	185
Grapes, purple, ½ cup	33	1 whole	370
green, ½ cup	48	Bamboo shoots, 1 cup	21
Grapefruit, 1 average	58	Bean Sprouts, ½ cup	16
Grape juice,		Beets, ½ cup cooked	20-23
unsweetened, 1 cup	155	Broccoli, ½ cup cooked	20-23
Honeydew melon,		Brussel sprouts,	
½ cup diced	40	½ cup cooked	23-25

Cabbage,		Tomato, 1 average	33
½ cup raw shredded, green	12	Watercress, 5-8 sprigs	3

Grains — Calories

Cabbage, ½ cup raw shredded, red	16
½ cup cooked	17
Carrots, 1 average	21
½ cup cooked	23
juice, 8 oz.	240
Cauliflower, ½ cup cooked	13
Celery, ½ cup diced	9
Chard, ½ cup cooked	14
Chives, fresh, 1 Tbsp.	3
Corn, 1 average ear	71
½ cup cooked	69
Cucumber, 1	29
½ lb., 2 cups slices	33
Eggplant, cooked ½ cup	19
Green Beans, ½ cup cooked	16
Lettuce, 3 large leaves	6
Mung bean sprouts, ½ cup	16
Mushrooms, ½ lb. (2 cups sliced)	61
Onion, 1 raw	40
cooked, ½ cup	30
Parsley, fresh ½ cup	11
Parsnips, cooked ½ cup	51
Peas, ½ cup	57
split peas cooked ½ cup	115
Peppers, 1 average green raw	14
½ cup green	10
1 average red	19
½ cup red	14
Pimientos, 4 oz	31
Potatoes, 1 small baked	93
1 medium baked	115
Steamed, ½ cup	55
Sweet, ½ cup	105
Sweet, 1 average	155
1 small boiled	76
Pumpkin, ½ lb.	42
canned ½ cup	38
seeds, 1 oz	155
Rhubarb, raw ½ lb	31
Scallion, 1	9
Snow peas, ½ cup	22
Soybean sprouts, raw ½ cup	25
Spinach, cooked ½ cup	16
Squash, zucchini, ½ cup	16
yellow, ½ cup	16
butternut, ½ cup	16
hubbard, ½ cup	50
acorn, cooked ½ cup	57
spaghetti, cooked ½ cup	58

Grains — Calories

Item	Calories
Bagel, 1 average	165
Barley, dry ½ cup	295
Bran, 1 cup	152
Breads, 1 average slice	100
bible,	171
chapati, 1	112
corn tortilla, 1	64
Dimpflmeier 100% rye plus - 1 slice	95
Essene, 1/16	80
English muffin, 2 halves	160
Oasis, 1 slice	110
Breadcrumbs, 1 Tbsp.	22
Cereal, Grape Nuts, 1 cup	400
All Bran, 1 cup	192
Cornmeal, ½ cup cooked	80
½ cup dry	212
Cracker crumbs, graham ½ cup	214
Cream or rice, ¾ cup cooked	95
Cream of wheat, ¾ cup cooked	100
Macaroni, ½ cup cooked	85
Millet, ½ cup cooked	102
Noodles, ½ cup cooked	96
Oatmeal, 1 cup cooked	108
Pancake, 1 four inch	60
Popcorn, plain, 1 cup popped	54
Rice, brown cooked ½ cup	100
wild, cooked ½ cup	100
Rice cake, round 1	35
square 1	20
Rice flour, 1 cup	479
Wholewheat flour, 1 cup	400

Dairy Products — Calories

Item	Calories
Butter, 1 Tbsp.	100
Cheese, Blue, 1 oz	103
Bleu, 4 oz. (1 cup)	400
Brick, 1 oz	100
Lowfat cottage, ½ cup	101
Dry curd Cottage, ½ cup	90
Lo-cal Jack, 1 oz	80
Mozzarella, 1 oz	79
Muenster cheese, 1 oz	100
Parmesan, 1 Tbsp.	33
Part Skim Ricotta, ¼ cup	68
Soy, 1 oz	78

Swiss, 1 oz	95	Kidneys, ½ cup cooked	109
Yogurt cheese, ¼ cup	48	Pintos, ½ cup cooked	140
Cheddar, 1 oz	111		

Miscellaneous	Calories
Cottage, creamed ½ cup	120		
uncreamed, ½ cup	98	Agar, 1 Tbsp.	2
Cream cheese, 1 oz	105	Arrowroot, 1 Tbsp.	29
Cream, sour 1 Tbsp.	26	Barbeque Sauce 1 oz	50
Cream,		Braggs, 1 Tbsp. liquid	9
heavy whipping 1 Tbsp.	53	aminos	
light whipping 1 Tbsp.	45	1 cup,	144
Gouda, 1 oz	108	Brown rice syrup, 1 Tbsp.	42
Half & Half, 1 Tbsp.	20	Carob powder, toasted, 1 cup	452
Milk, whole 8 oz.	159	Catsup, 1 Tbsp.	18
low fat, 1 cup	140	1 cup,	288
non-fat 1 cup	90	Cheese sauce, ½ cup	144
evaporated skim milk,	100	Coffee, 1 cup decaf	2
½ cup		Cornstarch, 1 Tbsp.	29
buttermilk, 8 oz	89	Fructose, 1 Tbsp.	48
powder, nonfat 1 cup	256	Honey, 1 Tbsp.	64
powder, dry whole 4 Tbsp.	142	Lecithin, liquid 1 Tbsp.	120
Yogurt,		Maple Syrup, 1 Tbsp.	120
from whole milk, 1 cup	153	Miso, red 1 Tbsp.	27
½ cup	77	Molasses, 1 Tbsp.	46
lowfat, 1 cup	144	Mustard, stoneground 1 oz	26

Nuts & Seeds	Calories
		Nori, 6 sheets	10
		Nutritional Yeast, 1 Tbsp.	23
Almond butter, 1 Tbsp.	100	Oil, 1 Tbsp. (can vary	125
Almonds, ½ cup	425	according to type)	
9-10 nuts	37	Olives, green, 1	5
Brazil nuts, ½ cup shelled	458	or 4 medium	15
4-5 nuts	98	black, 1	7
Cashews, 6-8 nuts	84	Pickles, 1 large dill	15
Coconut,		Raisins, ½ cup	231
½ cup unsweetened	340	Salad Dressing, 1 Tbsp.	85-100
Filberts, 10-12 nuts	95	Salsa, 1 Tbsp.	7
Macadamia, 6 nuts	104	Sauerkraut, ½ cup	21
Pecans, ½ cup halves	371	Sesame seeds, 1 Tbsp.	53
1 Tbsp. chopped	51	Spaghetti Sauce,	
Pinenuts, pignolia 1 Tbsp.	42	low cal, 1 cup	120
Sesame seeds, 1 oz whole	160	Tamari, 1 Tbsp.	9
Sunflower seeds, 1 oz	160	Tapioca pearls, 1 tsp.	30
1 Tbsp.	53	Tempeh, ½ lb.	380
Walnuts, ½ cup	314	Tofu, 1" sliced 2½" square	72
1 Tbsp. chopped	52	cheese, 1 oz	43
Nut butters, 1 Tbsp., varies	100	8 oz (1 cup)	344
according to manufacturer	ave.	Tomato Juice, 8 oz	46

Beans	Calories
		Tomato paste, 4 oz	93
		Tomato sauce, ½ cup	35
Black-eyed peas,		Vanilla, 1 tsp.	6
½ cup cooked	95	Vinegar, 1 Tbsp.	2
Green, ½ cup cooked	16	Water chestnuts, 16	80
Lentils, ½ cup cooked	106	Watercress, 5-8 sprigs	3
Limas, ½ cup cooked	95	White Sauce, ½ cup	148

INDEX